Plato's Re

CW01083785

Edinburgh Philosophical Guides Series

Plato's *Republic*

An Edinburgh Philosophical Guide

D. J. Sheppard

Edinburgh University Press

Edinburgh University Press Ltd
22 George Square, Edinburgh

www.euppublishing.com

Typeset in 11/13pt Monotype Baskerville by
Servis Filmsetting Ltd, Stockport, Cheshire, and
printed and bound by CPI Antony Rowe, Chippenham and Eastbourne

A CIP record for this book is available from the British Library

ISBN 978 0 7486 2778 3 (hardback)
ISBN 978 0 7486 2779 0 (paperback)

Contents

Series Editor's Preface

To us, the principle of this series of books is clear and simple: what readers new to philosophical classics need first and foremost is help with *reading* these key texts. That is to say, help with the often antique or artificial style, the twists and turns of arguments on the page, as well as the vocabulary found in many philosophical works. New readers also need help with those first few daunting and disorienting sections of these books, the point of which are not at all obvious. The books in this series take you through each text step-by-step, explaining complex key terms and difficult passages which help to illustrate the way a philosopher thinks in prose.

We have designed each volume in the series to correspond to the way the texts are actually taught at universities around the world, and have included helpful guidance on writing university-level essays or examination answers. Designed to be read alongside the text, our aim is to enable you to *read* philosophical texts with confidence and perception. This will enable you to make your own judgements on the texts, and on the variety of opinions to be found concerning them. We want you to feel able to join the great dialogue of philosophy, rather than remain a well-informed eavesdropper.

Douglas Burnham

Author's Preface

Yet another introductory guide to Plato's *Republic* requires some justification. In my view, the problem with the books available is that they
only succeed in introducing readers to the author's own interpretation of the *Republic*, considering alternative interpretative possibilities
merely as means to that end. To the extent that they accomplish this
task, a number of them are of considerable worth, and on a number
of points I shall refer to them. However, the great danger is that rather
than encouraging first-time readers to engage with the *Republic* for
themselves, they serve as 'ready to wear' substitutes for such an
engagement. To avoid this fate, in the commentary that follows I have
endeavoured to make as few interpretative decisions as possible,
instead offering a range of interpretative possibilities in order to help
readers develop their own response to Plato's text.

It would be naïve to suppose that I have remained wholly neutral
in this endeavour: to commentate is, of course, already to interpret.
Furthermore, from the overwhelming mass of secondary material on
the *Republic* I have had to decide which interpretative possibilities to
highlight. In this I have been guided by a number of sometimes competing considerations: those interpretations that have been the most
influential in recent decades; those that provide a suitable contrast
with one another (in the hope that this will help spur the reader into
a critical engagement with Plato's text); and those that are most
readily accessible to first-time readers in respect of style, content and
availability. In the number and identity of the exclusions that this
inevitably involves, the book is sure to disappoint many. In addition,
I have doubtless failed at various points to hide my own interpretative
preferences. Indeed, in some cases that failure is intended. Most con-
spicuously, I confess to a particular 'agenda' in respect of the common

thor's Preface

ion – especially at the introductory level – that the *Republic* is
ly a contribution to political philosophy. It is certainly not my
on to suggest that this assumption is mistaken; in what follows
olitical reading' in some of its manifold guises is presented as
of the principal interpretative possibilities on offer. But it is my
inion that the way in which a number of influential introductions
o the *Republic* adopt the political approach to the dialogue without
serious consideration of the alternatives serves to inhibit, rather than
to encourage, the critical encounter with Plato's dialogue that I aim
to facilitate.

In short, I have sought to write an introductory guide that does precisely that: introduces the first-time reader to the *Republic* – just as one might introduce a new friend to an old one – in an attempt to encourage them to begin their own conversation with Plato's text, rather than undertaking that conversation on the readers' behalf. If it succeeds in this, then the effort of writing it will have been worthwhile.

I wish to thank the editors of the *Richmond Journal of Philosophy* for permission to utilise material first published in 'On Why the Philosopher Returns to the Cave', from Issue 6, Spring 2004, and ' "A bit deaf and short-sighted": Plato's Critique of Democracy', from Issue 10, Summer 2005.

I have contracted a significant number of intellectual debts since I first read Plato as an undergraduate at the University of Warwick, but those owed to Martin Warner, Christine Battersby, Andrew Benjamin, Stephen Houlgate, Angela Hobbes, and Greg Hunt stand out. I cannot mention my time at Warwick without acknowledging my gratitude to Colin Thomas, a friend indeed. At Staffordshire University, I was fortunate enough to work with Douglas Burnham and David Webb, who set standards of intellectual generosity that I have subsequently endeavoured to follow, albeit without their success. I should also like to thank Haydn Curran for his friendship and support during my time at Kenilworth School. I have written most of this book since arriving at Oakham School, where I have benefitted immensely from the companionship of Crispin Dawson, Anthony Macpherson, Douglas Leckie, and Jennifer Gillett, and the support of the Headmaster, Joseph Spence, who brought me to the school. There are also the students at the aforementioned institutions, conversations with whom have helped me decide what is required of an introduction to the *Republic*.

I should never have written this book without the love and support of my wife, Annadolores, and my son, Spencer. The book is dedicated to them.

Oakham, 2008

1. Introductory Questions

This chapter will consider some of questions commonly asked by readers new to Plato's *Republic*. It is a source of frustration to some that these seemingly straightforward questions do not permit straightforward answers, but their simplicity is deceiving; they touch on controversial matters that have a fundamental bearing on how the *Republic* is interpreted.

One question concerns the historical context in which the *Republic* is read at the beginning of the twenty-first century. It is often ignored in introductory books that exclusively focus on the context in which the *Republic* was written. If for no other reason, however, it speaks to the basic question of why I have written this book and why you are reading it:

What is so Important about the *Republic*?

For many, the study of the *Republic* – or at least parts of it – forms their introduction to Plato, if not to philosophy itself. Further, when Plato is first discussed in the context of classical civilisation, political theory, ethics, art and literature, psychology, education or theology, attention will most likely focus on the *Republic*. The question is why, of all Plato's dialogues, it is the *Republic* that has come to occupy this privileged position, both in relation to its author's *oeuvre* and the Western intellectual tradition as a whole.

We have already alluded to one answer that speaks to both contexts. The *Republic* considers many of the central preoccupations of Western thought: justice, happiness and the good life; truth and the distinction between knowledge and opinion; the relation between physical and metaphysical realms; human psychology; the nature and purpose of education; the ideal form of government and the value of democracy; the place of philosophy in society; the definition and value of art, and so on. To adapt Samuel Johnson's phrase, when one is tired of the *Republic*, one is tired of philosophical reflection itself. Yet it is not by some happy coincidence that the *Republic* examines many of the fundamental concerns in Western philosophy. To a significant extent, it is precisely *because* Plato examined them in the *Republic* – and elsewhere in his work – that they subsequently preoccupied his successors. A. N. Whitehead's remark that 'the safest characterisation of the European philosophical tradition is that it consists of a series of footnotes to Plato' overstates the matter, but it contains a kernel of truth (Whitehead 1929: 135). And whilst it is the case that many of the topics considered in the *Republic* are examined elsewhere in Plato's works, in the *Republic* they are considered in the course of a single, extended discussion. Therefore, it is hardly surprising that the *Republic* is adopted as an introduction to philosophy in general and/or an introduction to Plato in particular, and that other disciplines look to it in the first instance.

Nonetheless, it would be wrong to suppose that the *Republic* has always held its current pre-eminence. This is important to recognise, since the story of the rise of the *Republic* reveals much about the interpretative context in which it continues to be read today.

There is little evidence that the *Republic* held a special place amongst Plato's works in the ancient world. When the systematic exposition of Plato's philosophy became the trend, it was the *Timaeus*, a dialogue on cosmology, which was viewed as the key work. With the dissolution of the Western Roman Empire, the *Timaeus* became the only Platonic dialogue that was known in any detail in the West, and serious study of Plato became the almost exclusive preserve of the Islamic tradition. In medieval Europe, Aristotle was the pre-eminent ancient philosopher, exerting an enormous influence on the philosophical culture of the time. Thus, when Dante, writing in the early fourteenth century, describes the fate of the ancient Greek philosophers in *The Divine Comedy*, there is no need to refer to Aristotle by name; the soubriquet 'the master of them that know' suffices, with Plato and Socrates sitting at his feet, honouring him (Dante 1995: 75–6).

It is instructive to compare this representation with Raphael's *School of Athens*, painted at the beginning of the sixteenth century, in which

Plato and Aristotle are granted equal status. In the meantime, Plato has returned to prominence as a result of the Renaissance revival in classical learning. The Florentine philosopher Marsilio Ficino has translated all of Plato's known works into Latin for the first time, including the *Republic*, and it is no longer eccentric for the likes of Ficino to describe Plato as 'the father of philosophers' (Ficino 2001: 9). Yet it is notable that Raphael's Plato holds a copy of the *Timaeus*. While the *Republic* is once again being read in the West, it is typically viewed as a political fantasy; the model for works such as Thomas More's *Utopia* (1516). The *Timaeus* retains its central place in the Platonic canon.

The current reputation of the *Republic* is largely a legacy of the nineteenth century. Following a period of relative neglect, scholarly attention was again paid to Plato in Germany during the early nineteenth century. The first English translation of Plato's works by Thomas Taylor was also published at this time. A number of interpretative approaches to Plato developed, among them the approach pioneered by the influential German philosopher Friedrich Schleiermacher, who viewed the *Republic* as a late work, and as such the culmination of Plato's intellectual development. 'This splendid structure,' he wrote, 'contains, as it were, built into its foundations, the keystones of all those noble arches on which [Plato's philosophy] rests' (Schleiermacher 1974: 179). Schleiermacher's estimation of the *Republic* was not restricted to those who shared his 'developmental' approach to Plato. The British philosopher George Grote was inclined to treat the dialogues as discrete entities that resisted systematisation. Still he judged the *Republic* 'undoubtedly the grandest of all [Plato's] compositions; including in itself all his different points of excellence' (Grote 1973: IV, 95).

The scholarly vanguard aside, it took time for Plato's pre-eminence – and with it both Schleiermacher and Grote's estimations of the *Republic* – to become entrenched. To take the situation in Britain, as late as 1834 we find John Stuart Mill relating an anecdote about a bookseller whose inability to sell an edition of Plato's dialogues is a major cause of his bankruptcy, and speculating that in Britain there are 'not so many as a hundred persons who have ever read Plato' (cited in Burnyeat 1998: 355). Yet by 1866, the translation of the *Republic* by John Llewelyn Davies and David James Vaughan was in its third edition as part of the popular 'Golden Treasury' series – it was first published in 1852 – the translators confidently acclaiming it as Plato's 'acknowledged masterpiece' (cited in Burnyeat 1998: 368).

At least as significantly, under the aegis of Benjamin Jowett, Regius Professor of Greek and later Vice-Chancellor of Oxford University, the *Republic* became a prescribed text on the Oxford 'Greats' syllabus in 1872. The Ficino of his day – he translated all of Plato's dialogues into English more or less single-handedly – Jowett was responsible for institutionalising the view of the *Republic* as 'certainly the greatest' of the dialogues and 'the centre around which the other dialogues may be grouped' (Jowett 1921: 1). He also expressed the still prevalent view that the central sections of the *Republic* – specifically Books V–VII, which contain an exposition of the so-called 'theory of the forms' and the analogy of the cave – constitute the apex not only of Plato's philosophy, but also of ancient thought as a whole. Lastly, in the modern epoch it is Jowett who popularised the view of the *Republic* as an important contribution to political philosophy.

Two issues dominated intellectual debate in Britain at the middle of the nineteenth century: the threats to traditional Christian belief posed by Charles Darwin's evolutionary account of creation and the historical criticism of the Bible, and the question of political governance in a country transformed by the Industrial Revolution. In Plato's thought as a whole, Jowett perceived a means of shoring up traditional moral values in the face of increased scepticism of religion, and in the *Republic* in particular he perceived a model for how the modern state might be organised. According to Jowett, Plato's proposals for the ideal city provided the template for a liberal meritocracy in which the right to rule was based on ability rather than inheritance. Moreover, in Plato's vision of the 'philosopher-ruler' Jowett saw an ideal of disinterested duty that he hoped would inspire those who read the *Republic* at university to devote themselves to public service rather than the pursuit of wealth.

Jowett's focus on the political aspects of the *Republic* survived into the twentieth century, though in the eyes of many, Plato the Victorian meritocrat was recast as Plato the totalitarian. Richard Crossman and Karl Popper, writing in the 1930s and 1940s respectively, viewed Plato's ideal city as the forerunner of Hitler's Germany and Stalin's

Russia, Popper famously declaring that 'Plato's political programme, far from being morally superior to totalitarianism, is fundamentally identical with it' (Popper 1995: 93).

The perception of the *Republic* as a political work endured throughout the twentieth century and has persisted into our own (discussion of Popper's critique remains a staple of examination papers on the *Republic*). In the popular mind, the *Republic* is best known as the dialogue that contains Plato's vision of an ideal city ruled by philosophers. As we have seen, a number of factors explain the perceived pre-eminence of the *Republic*, but its reputation as an important contribution to political philosophy is one of the foremost among them.

In drawing attention to this reputation, it is not my intention to suggest that it is mistaken. As we shall see, there is much to be said for it. (In the first instance, one might point to the title of the dialogue itself. The English title derives from the Latin translation – *res publica* – of the Greek title *Politeia*, which means something like 'political business' or 'the public and political life of the community'.) Nor do I draw attention to it in order to make a broader relativist point that all interpretations of the *Republic* are prisoners of their particular historical context, and that no interpretation can be judged more valuable than another. My purpose is to encourage readers to examine the matter for themselves, rather than simply accepting the critical assumptions of the age without demur. The view of the *Republic* as a political work is an excellent example of an interpretative disposition which is so entrenched that the assumptions on which it is based are rarely scrutinised, not least in introductory texts. Indeed, at this stage the reader may be wondering what the alternative disposition could possibly be. Further, having considered the alternative, the reader may yet conclude that the *Republic* is best read as a contribution to political philosophy. Ushering the reader in one interpretative direction rather than another on any point of interpretation is not the purpose of this book. Rather, my aim is to ensure that whatever conclusion is decided, it is not for the want of an awareness of at least some of the other interpretative possibilities (in the present context – to which we shall return – the view that the principal focus of the dialogue is ethical rather than political).

We do not leave this matter behind in turning to our second question:

Who is Plato?

Curiosity concerning Plato's biography is heightened by the fact that Plato never speaks in his own name in the dialogues. However, whilst legends abound, verifiable facts are few and far between.

We cannot even be certain that 'Plato' was Plato's name. Among the various and conflicting biographical sources, there is one tradition according to which 'Plato' was a nickname and his real name was Aristocles. This is no more or less credible than many of the anecdotes about Plato's life. We do know that Aristocles was the name of Plato's paternal grandfather, and that naming the eldest son for the father's father was common practice. But we cannot be certain that Plato was the eldest son, whilst we do know that Plato was a relatively common name at the time, and as such rather more of the order of 'Joe' than of a nickname like 'bookworm' or 'big ears'. 'Plato', incidentally, is close to *platus*, meaning 'broad', and one explanation in the ancient sources is that the nickname stuck because Plato was a wrestler renowned for his broad shoulders. The moral of the story is to treat claims to biographical certainty with caution, not least when they are used to corroborate a particular interpretation of the *Republic*.

We can be reasonably certain that Plato was born in Athens in 427 BC, and that he died in 347 BC. Since the defeat of the Persians at the battles of Marathon in 490 BC and of Salamis in 479 BC, Athens had led an alliance of 'city-states' that was the dominant power in the Mediterranean region. But Athens ultimately overreached itself, and by 431 BC was embroiled in a mutually debilitating conflict – the Great Peloponnesian War – with an alliance led by Sparta. Plato was four or five when an armistice was agreed between Athens and Sparta in 423 BC – the 'Peace of Nicias' followed in 421 BC – by the terms of which it seemed that Athens might retain its empire. However, as the Greek historian Thucydides observes, it was a 'festering peace', and it ended in 415 BC when Athens decided to send a fleet to Sicily. The fleet was destroyed at Syracuse in 413 BC, and the end of its naval supremacy dealt a massive blow to Athenian hopes. Still the fighting continued for almost another decade, and it was only with the help of Persian money that Sparta ultimately prevailed, following the battle of Aegospotami in 405 BC, and a successful blockade of the Hellespont, a vital supply route to Athens, in 404 BC.

Plato was in his early twenties when the war ended. He belonged to an aristocratic and well connected family, and it is difficult to imagine that his attitudes were not affected either by his social position or by the period of upheaval and decline that he experienced. But precisely how they affected him is unknown. We do know that Plato's family was involved in the civil strife that followed the defeat in 404 BC. After the death of his father, Ariston, Plato's mother, Perictione, had married Pyrilampes, a keen supporter of Athenian democracy. At the same time, Perictione's brother, Critias, and his cousin, Charmides, were both involved in an anti-democratic coup that brought to power a group known as 'the Thirty' – or 'Thirty Tyrants' – who ruled until the restoration of democracy in 399 BC. However, we do not know on which side Plato stood in this conflict, or if he was involved in any particular way.

We would be in a better position to speculate if we knew that the *Seventh Letter* was genuine. It is one of thirteen letters purportedly by Plato that have come down to us along with his other works. Most are thought to be by other hands – writing such letters in the style of someone else was a common exercise – but it is often claimed that the *Seventh Letter* is by Plato. It tells of how his initial high hopes for the regime of the Thirty were soon dashed, and how events under the restored democracy – not least the trial and death of Socrates – resulted in a lasting disillusionment with Athenian politics. The bulk of the letter is then taken up with an account of three trips to Sicily made by Plato at the behest of his friend, Dion, in an ultimately fruitless effort to persuade Dionysus, the tyrannical ruler of Syracuse, to adopt Plato's proposals for political reform along the lines suggested in the *Republic*. In addition, the story is usually told that at some point between or after these unsuccessful visits, Plato established what became known as the Academy – after the suburb of Athens in which it was located, sacred to the hero *Academus* – a school of philosophy that he led until his death.

The issue of the reliability of the *Seventh Letter* as a record of Plato's life and attitudes is important, since it is often used to corroborate the view that the *Republic* is its author's response to the political turmoil in Athens. Further, it is thought to reflect a political idealism that Plato would subsequently reject in the wake of his failure in Sicily, resulting in the very different political proposals advanced in his final work, the *Laws*.

I have nothing to contribute to the debate over the authenticity of the *Seventh Letter*. In the present context, the stance adopted by Julia Annas seems the most sensible: 'given what we have,' she writes, 'the reasonable course is to suspend judgement' (Annas 1999: 77). Consequently, in what follows I shall not rely on the evidence of the *Seventh Letter* to support the political approach to the *Republic* in the manner of some other introductions. I reiterate the point that, in so doing, the aim is not to undermine the political approach; it is simply to avoid prejudging the matter and to encourage readers to develop their own responses based on the evidence of the *Republic* itself.

Different biographical issues arise in answering our next question:

Who is Socrates?

For our purposes there are two Socrates: the historical Socrates – c. 468 BC–399 BC – and the fictional Socrates who is the principal speaker in most of Plato's dialogues, not least the *Republic*. It is essential to differentiate between them.

Let us begin with the historical figure. As with Plato's biography, facts are thin on the ground, since few contemporary sources survive. The most notable absence is anything by Socrates himself, though we can be reasonably certain that this is because he did not write anything. Therefore, our view of Socrates is filtered through the views of others: we have the Socrates who appears in Plato's dialogues; the Socrates who is the subject of Xenophon's writings; a very different portrait in Aristophanes' play, *The Clouds*; and a handful of other fragments.

We know that Socrates' origins were less exalted than Plato's, but although he is often said to have died a poor man, we have no reason to believe that he was born into poverty. His father is thought to have been a stonemason, and if it is true that Socrates served as a 'hoplite' – a member of the heavy infantry – then a certain level of prosperity is indicated, in that hoplites had to provide their own weapons and armour. Nevertheless, it is not obvious that Socrates possessed a steady source of income, since he was supposed never to have charged for his teaching. He did marry a woman called Xanthippe, an aristocratic name that may offer a clue as to how Socrates made ends meet, but whatever the truth of the matter he was notorious for adopting a very ascetic lifestyle. In Plato's *Symposium*, Alcibiades recounts Socrates' great bravery during his military service in the Peloponnesian War, adding that even in the depths of winter he wore 'the same old coat' and walked barefoot in the ice (*Symposium*, 220a–b).

In *The Clouds* Aristophanes too mentions Socrates' habit of going barefoot. First performed in 423 BC, *The Clouds* is central to our understanding of Socrates' biography, not so much for the insights that it contains into Socrates' character – it is generally believed to offer a caricature rather than a realistic portrait – but because it attests to the conviction that, by the late 420s, Socrates had become a sufficiently controversial figure to be satirised in popular drama. Aristophanes' Socrates is the head of a ramshackle institution professing to teach its students how to prevail in discussion using the weaker argument, principally so that they can avoid having to pay their debts. Socrates is presented as a corrupt and corrupting character with dangerous moral and religious views. There is little evidence that it is an accurate representation. For example, it is inconceivable that Socrates presided over anything like a school or university, since he was one of a number of peripatetic teachers – known collectively as 'sophists' – who offered their services to wealthy Athenian families for the purposes of preparing their sons for roles in public life. Further, Socrates appears to have differed from the majority of his peers not only in refusing payment for his services, but in insisting on a pursuit of truth that was at odds with the exigencies of preparation for a life in politics. This is certainly suggested by Plato, and it is corroborated at least in part by Xenophon. Indeed, if we assume that Plato's portrayal of Socrates as an unorthodox, uncompromising, and somewhat eccentric figure is closer to reality, then it is not so difficult to see how Aristophanes' comic portrayal of Socrates as a subversive misfit might emerge in reaction and strike a chord with a suspicious public.

It is interesting that *Clouds* exploits Socrates' reputation for holding unconventional religious views, since impiety seems to have been one of the charges brought against Socrates in 399 BC by an influential group of citizens under the restored democracy. We do not know the precise reason for the accusation, which probably included the charge of corrupting the youth of Athens through his teaching, though it may have been driven by political as well as religious motivations.

Socrates appears to have adopted an apolitical stance during the turmoil in Athens, possessing friends and associates on both sides of the political divide, though it may be that his association with the likes of Charmides and Critias – both members of the Thirty – ultimately counted for more than his friendship with prominent democrats such as Lysias and Chaerephon. Socrates was convicted by his fellow citizens and sentenced to death, his execution immortalised – and most probably idealised – by Plato in *Crito*, with Socrates self-administering the dose of hemlock that ended his life.

In death, Socrates remained an iconic figure and to many an intellectual hero, the desire to commemorate him spawning an entire genre of what Aristotle labelled 'Socratic conversations'. Of these, only Plato's and Xenophon's efforts have survived, except for the odd reference in other sources. Indeed, there is no greater testament to Socrates' effect on Plato, and the esteem in which the latter held him, than Plato's adoption of Socrates as the principal speaker in the majority of his dialogues, including the *Republic*. However, this begs a question that draws the 'other' Socrates into the equation, namely:

Are the Historical Socrates and Plato's Socrates One and the Same?

The belief that Plato adopted Socrates as the principal speaker in many of his dialogues as an act of homage is relatively uncontroversial. Far more contentious is the extent to which the views expressed by Plato's Socrates are those of the historical Socrates. It is a question often raised by those new to Plato, but while of undoubted historical interest, it is tempting to treat it rather cursorily. First of all, it is a hopelessly speculative debate, since we have nothing in Socrates' own hand against which to check the veracity of Plato's account. Second, its relevance to our present concerns is highly questionable aside from the opportunity it provides to discount the view that the *Republic* is a verbatim record of a Socratic conversation. (We possess nothing to suggest that this is what any practitioner of the Socratic conversation sought to accomplish, not least Plato.) Perhaps if we were undertaking a comparison between two or more of Plato's works, then it might be relevant to ask which of them was more or less influenced by Socrates' own ideas. But our focus is the *Republic* alone, and so the consideration does not apply.

The matter cannot be wholly ignored, however, since it pertains to a broader controversy regarding the chronology of Plato's dialogues. This is relevant to our concerns because the place allocated to the *Republic* in Plato's development has had a considerable impact on its interpretation. The issue of the relation between the historical and the fictional Socrates thrives on this debate. The construction of a historical Socrates from the evidence afforded by Plato's Socrates depends on the assumption that it is possible to determine a period in Plato's development during which he remained in the thrall of certain Socratic doctrines.

We have no reliable external evidence about the order in which Plato wrote the dialogues beyond Aristotle's insistence that the *Republic* preceded the *Laws*. Nevertheless, since the nineteenth century it has been common practice to believe that the statistical analysis of stylistic features in Plato's writing – 'stylometry' – offers an insight into the order of their composition, enabling us to distinguish between early, middle and late stages in Plato's development. By the terms of this division, the *Republic* is usually placed among the dialogues of Plato's 'middle' period (by which time, incidentally, he is supposed to have shaken free of the direct influence of Socrates). One of the consequences of this designation is again to bolster the perception of the *Republic* as a political work, specifically the product of a confident and idealistic period in Plato's intellectual life that ended with the author's adventures in Sicily. The 'middle' period designation also has a bearing on the debate concerning the status of the early sections of the *Republic*, as we shall see.

In recent years, however, the habits ingrained by stylometric research have been questioned. For example, doubt has been cast on whether we should view the 'middle' dialogues as arriving in the middle of Plato's development simply because the 'aporetic' works – shorter dialogues in which no specific conclusion is reached – must precede the 'constructive' works in which Plato's Socrates advances positive doctrines (as is often supposed to be the case in the *Republic*). Further, the reliability of the stylometric data as a guide to Plato's development has been called into question. It is suggested that at any time in his career Plato might have mimicked his earlier style, raising the possibility that a supposedly early dialogue might in fact be late. Lastly, even if the stylometric data is accurate and gives us an idea of the chronology, what it is able to tell us about Plato's development is limited since we know so little about why and for whom the dialogues were written. Efforts to meet these objections have also been made. It is said that reservations about the stylometric data are misguided, and that the data can indeed be relied on as a guide to Plato's development. Further, it is claimed that, notwithstanding certain qualms about its veracity, a broad consensus on the chronology of the dialogues is necessary if scholarly discussion of them is not to lose itself in a morass of conflicting impressions. (For both sides of the argument, see Annas and Rowe 2002.)

The debate will doubtless continue. It is brought to the reader's attention since in many interpretations of the *Republic*, claims relying at least in part on assumptions about its place in Plato's development remain undeclared, or they are asserted as incontrovertible facts. It is another issue on which we shall suspend judgement, avoiding any interpretative judgements that assume the *Republic* to be a 'middle' dialogue. (Again, since we are to examine the text in isolation, there are few consequences of doing that.) To conclude, we do not know the relation between the historical Socrates and Plato's Socrates, but this ignorance has little substantive bearing on how the *Republic* is read as a philosophical rather than as a historical document. For all intents and purposes, our focus is on the Platonic Socrates who appears in the *Republic*.

And yet, in dismissing the possibility that Plato was simply Socrates' amanuensis and adopted the dialogue form in order to transcribe actual Socratic conversations, a new question emerges:

Why did Plato Write Dialogues?

Readers new to Plato regularly ask this question, wondering why Plato did not adopt the treatise or essay as the means of expounding his ideas. The short answer is that we do not know; the consequence of that is a good deal of scholarly speculation on the matter. Today it is almost unheard of for a philosopher to present a book to a publisher, less still an essay to an academic journal, in the form of a dramatic dialogue. There would need to be a very specific rationale for doing so, and even then it would most likely be considered an eccentric choice. But it would be wrong to suppose that a similar situation existed in the fourth century BC. It is easily forgotten that for Plato and his original audience the 'Socratic conversation' was not so unusual at all. As we have already observed, a number of Socrates' associates adopted the dialogue form, and we might reasonably suppose they did so with a view to honouring the memory of their mentor. The debate is over whether this is all we can sensibly speculate about Plato's particular decision to write dialogues.

I shall outline two broadly – and therefore rather artificially – conceived answers to this question, though there are innumerable variations on their respective themes (see Griswold 1988). The reader would be mistaken to suppose that this is a mildly diverting but ultimately marginal question to be raised in passing before proceeding to the dialogue itself. How it is answered has significant implications for how the *Republic* is read.

The Dialogue as a Vehicle for Plato's Philosophy

This response is disinclined to stray too far from the idea that Plato adopted the dialogue form as an act of homage to Socrates. In its modern incarnation, it is often associated with 'analytic' interpretations of Plato, though in its original impulse it might be traced back to the 'doctrinal' or 'dogmatic' tradition of reading Plato current in antiquity.

According to this approach, since the medium of Socrates' philosophical practice was the 'live' conversation rather than the written treatise, so the dramatic dialogue is the appropriate means of commemorating Socrates. However, Plato is not merely Socrates' disciple but a philosopher in his own right, and in time develops his own position. Still, he retains the dialogue form, for one or a number of reasons. First, the written dialogue is a compromise between, on one hand, the need to write in order to preserve, and, on the other, Plato's commitment to Socrates' view that dialogical conversation is the key to true learning. Second, Plato does not want his audience to accept the philosophical theses expounded in the dialogues simply on his authority. Thus, the dialogue form makes it possible for Plato to present his ideas in the voice of another – in the *Republic*, as elsewhere, Socrates – encouraging readers to secure their own understanding. To this end, the dialogue form allows Plato to anticipate and respond to possible counter-arguments placed in the mouths of Socrates' interlocutors, further clarifying the argument (see Kraut 1992b).

An additional suggestion takes account of the view that Plato was 'inventing' philosophy as a new discipline. Plato recognised the distance separating the philosophical discourse that he envisaged from the conventional types of discourse to which his audience were accustomed. He could not refer his audience to an established philosophical language since none existed. But the dramatic dialogue provided the perfect means of closing the gap, enabling Plato to stage a conversation that takes as its starting point the non-philosophical position of Socrates' interlocutor, who is then drawn over to Socrates' – that is to say, Plato's – philosophical position in the course of the discussion. As we shall see, the opening pages of the *Republic* might be viewed as a case in point (see Rowe 2006).

These suggestions have much to commend them. Importantly, their underlying assumption is that the purpose of a dialogue is to articulate a particular set of philosophical doctrines, and those doctrines are to be specifically located in the words of the principal speaker, almost invariably Socrates. Consequently, the comparison between the Platonic dialogue and the plays of Greek tragedians such as Aeschylus, Sophocles and Aristophanes is misguided. The latter aim to produce an aesthetic effect; to this end it is perfectly proper for the main characters to utter opinions that are inimical to the author's own. But Plato aims to guide the reader to the truth, so it would be strange, if not deceitful, for his principal character to utter views that did not reflect his own.

The central implication of this answer to why Plato wrote dialogues is to license the reader to proceed on the proviso that *Socrates speaks for Plato*. The result is generally that less significance is paid to the dramatic aspects of the dialogue. Where the character of one or other participant might be said to illuminate Socrates' argument on a given point, then these are to be taken into account. Ultimately, however, Socrates' pronouncements are the focus of attention, since they allow us direct access to what Plato would have us think. It is often argued that there is no clearer justification for such an approach than the *Republic*, since once the reader is past the opening section, contributions by anyone other than Socrates are generally limited to the 'I quite agree, Socrates' variety. In summary, Socrates is Plato's mouthpiece, and while not treatises as such, the dialogues are most profitably read as though they shared many of the aims of the treatise.

Perhaps the principal attraction of this view is its simplicity. As we have said, it enables the reader to set aside the 'merely literary' aspects of the dialogue in order to concentrate on its 'properly philosophical' content. Further, it eases the way for comparative readings both across Plato's dialogues – of the type 'Plato says *x* in the *Republic* and the *Meno*, but *y* in the *Gorgias* – and between Plato and other philosophers – of the type 'Plato argues *x*, but Aristotle argues *y*'. Lastly, it is a practical matter if, with a view to focusing on certain themes in Plato's *oeuvre* – the 'theory of the forms', for example – only certain sections of a given dialogue are to be studied.

However, the counter-position complains that this is not so much simple as simplistic, encouraging a textually insensitive 'cut and paste' approach to Plato by which passages are torn from their proper context and held to represent 'Plato's philosophy' at this or that stage in his development. Opponents maintain that the 'Plato's mouthpiece' hypothesis is hugely presumptuous, based on a different conception of why Plato adopted the dialogue form.

The Dialogue as an Invitation to Philosophise

In its various contemporary guises – and there are many – this answer is generally associated with 'continental' readings of Plato, influenced by often competing positions within the twentieth-century German phenomenological and hermeneutical traditions. However, it too might be said to possess an ancient antecedent in the 'sceptical' tradition of reading Plato.

It is not hostile to the notion that Plato adopted the dialogue form in honour of Socrates, but it tends to take its point of departure from a different conception of the Socratic inheritance. Rather than a Socrates identified with particular doctrines, it inclines towards a Socrates who, as in Plato's *Apology*, knows only that he does not know (see *Apology*, 20d–23c). It is from this sceptical and ironical Socrates, who stands not for a body of philosophical doctrine so much as a certain philosophical practice, that Plato inherits. For as Socrates' scepticism and irony distance him from what he says, provoking a dialogical response from his interlocutor, so the dialogue form, in which Plato never speaks in his own name, distances him from what he writes, with a similar intention to provoke the reader into a dialogical engagement.

On one view, Plato's rationale for using the dialogue form to guarantee this distance between the author and what he writes is that he does not have any doctrines to impart; the dialogues are to be understood as open-ended thought experiments that unfold dialectically over their course, with preliminary conclusions transformed by those that succeed them; dramatic exercises designed as an invitation to philosophical reflection. Thus conceived, the comparison between the Platonic dialogue and other dramatic forms is for the most part appropriate. To read a dialogue is not to isolate the pronouncements of the principal character to the detriment of the dramatic aspects of the drama, but to view it as a philosophical and literary whole.

By no means is every scholar who understands Plato's adoption of the dialogue form in these terms as sceptical of Plato's doctrinal designs on his audience. Yet significantly, this does not lead back to the view that the dialogues are, in effect, barely disguised treatises. The dialogues are not simply disinterested thought experiments intended solely to draw the reader into the philosophical process, while at the same time the author's intentions are not automatically identified with the pronouncements of a particular character. Plato's rationale for adopting the dialogue form remains that of guaranteeing his anonymity with a view to providing a 'stage', so to speak, on which certain philosophical questions can be explored. But he does possess a position of his own, which emerges from the interaction of all of the speakers, within a certain context, over the course of the drama. In Stanley Rosen's words, 'Plato speaks in the story he tells, not in the arguments he assigns to his dramatic personae' (Rosen 2005: 2).

The central implication of this understanding of the dialogue form for how we read the *Republic* is to reject the assumption that Socrates is Plato's mouthpiece; we cannot simply read off Plato's doctrines from Socrates' words. Further, we cannot simply assume that inconsistencies in the text are matters of which Plato is necessarily unaware; perhaps they are part of a broader dramatic design. In the hands of the most able scholars, the results are some very imaginative and multi-layered readings that interweave the different philosophical and literary elements contained in the dialogues.

Since it tends to view each dialogue as its own self-contained philosophical drama, this approach is much less inclined to read 'across' dialogues, comparing what Socrates says in one dialogue with what he says elsewhere in an effort to piece together 'Plato's philosophy'. Likewise, it is resistant to the idea of studying only selected extracts from a dialogue, since to do so tends to marginalise the dramatic aspects of the whole. This reluctance goes some way to explaining its limited influence on the general reception of Plato, to speak of the English-speaking world, since the temptation to isolate choice extracts from a given dialogue is strong, especially when the dialogue is as long as the *Republic*. But there are other reasons why many Plato scholars reject the approach.

I mentioned that it has produced some inventive interpretations of the *Republic*. To its critics, however, what is a wonderfully imaginative reading to others is an exercise in untrammelled speculation to them. The objection is if the message the author is intending to convey is not contained in the words of one character, but is to be pieced together from all its various dramatic and philosophical elements, licence is given to all manner of disparate interpretations, as this or that meaning is imputed to various aspects of the text. To abandon the assumption that Socrates speaks for Plato, it is argued, causes the interpretative debate to collapse into a babble of competing voices (see Kraut 1992b).

As is clear, the difference between those who do and those who do not assume that Socrates is Plato's mouthpiece is fundamental and far-reaching. Consequently, it is perhaps unsurprising that, when it occurs, debate between advocates of the two approaches is often fractious in nature – so much so, that the temptation in an introductory text is to ignore the issue and simply assume one or other approach with little or no discussion. However, having brought the matter to the reader's attention, in what follows I shall endeavour to take account of both approaches where adopting one or other position has significant interpretative implications. To do otherwise would be to read the *Republic* on the reader's behalf.

A Note on References and Translation

References to Plato's works cite what are known as 'Stephanus pages'. Stephanus is the Latinised form of the surname Etienne. In 1578, the Parisian publisher and scholar Henri Etienne produced the first printed edition of Plato's works in the original Greek. We still use the page numbers together with the subdivision of 'a' to 'e' adopted by Stephanus – for example, '354a' – to refer to Plato's works both in ancient Greek and across the various translations. Consequently, whichever translation is used, it is possible to locate a given passage. (In what follows, all Stephanus references are to the *Republic*, unless another dialogue is specified. There is a similar system to facilitate reference to Aristotle's works, named after Immanuel Bekker's Greek edition of Aristotle published in 1831. Accordingly, whenever one of Aristotle's works is cited, it is to the name of the relevant text followed by the 'Bekker page' that reference will be made.)

As to the best English translation of the *Republic*, it is largely a matter of personal preference often based on extended acquaintance. Many retain a fondness for Desmond Lee's translation, whilst others are loyal to translations by Allan Bloom, G. M. A. Grube – in C. D. C. Reeve's revision – and Robin Waterfield, among others. I have been particularly impressed by Tom Griffith's recent translation, and it is this that I have followed for the most part (see the Bibliography and Guide to Further Reading for full details).

The reader will also notice that editions of the *Republic* are often divided into ten 'books', which in roman numerals are sometimes used to prefix Stephanus references. This convention predates Stephanus by many centuries, and appears to have been determined as much by the amount of text that fitted onto a single roll of papyrus as by a thematic break in the content of the dialogue itself. Commentaries on the *Republic* often refer to such and such an argument contained in 'Book V', for example, though for the purpose of referencing particular passages in essays and the like, the Stephanus page together with the subdivision will generally suffice. However, when reading from the ancient Greek, the convention is to add the specific line in question (for example, '354a2').

2. A Guide to the Text

Book I (327a–354c)

Book I of the *Republic* runs from 327a to 354c. Its structure and content stand in marked contrast to the remainder of the dialogue, and beg the question of its purpose in relation to the *Republic* as a whole. This matter will be addressed in due course. We shall begin by considering the opening scene, and outlining possible interpretations of its significance, before proceeding to Socrates' discussions with his three interlocutors: Cephalus, Polemarchus, and Thrasymachus.

The Opening Scene (327a–328b)

What is to be made of the beginning of the dialogue? Observe that, strictly speaking, the *Republic* is not a dialogue at all, but a first-person narrative in which Socrates relates a conversation that took place the previous day. No identity is assigned to Socrates' addressee. It is as though Socrates were speaking directly to the reader; as though one had just asked, 'So, Socrates, what happened to you yesterday?' With the opening line the latter's reply commences: 'I went down yesterday to the Piraeus with Glaucon' (327a). The tale is long in the telling.

Observe further that Socrates spends a good few lines setting the scene. We learn that he visited 'the Piraeus' – then as now the port of Athens, six miles to the west of the city and connected to it by walls – in the company of 'Glaucon, son of Ariston'. He was there to witness the festival of the Thracian moon goddess, Bendis, being celebrated in Athens for the first time. In passing, Socrates remarks that he was impressed by the local and Thracian contributions to the festivities. Having turned for home, he then relates that they were waylaid by a slave belonging to Polemarchus, and requested to wait. Polemarchus

approached, and in the course of a short exchange he persuaded
Socrates to delay returning to Athens and accompany him home.
There they met a number of others, including Polemarchus' father,
Cephalus, an old acquaintance of Socrates whom he had not seen for
some time, and with whom he quickly fell into conversation.

For many readers, it is only when the conversation with Cephalus
commences that the text begins in earnest, since it is only now that
the dialogue takes on a recognisably philosophical character. On this
view, Socrates' scene setting can be ignored for the most part, since
what are important are, in Nicholas White's words, 'ideas and arguments rather than the characterisations or other dramatic and literary elements' (White 1979: 62). The concern is that attention paid to
the latter distracts attention from the former. As we have seen,
however, this begs a fundamental question about Plato's reasons for
adopting the dialogue form. Broadly speaking, White's attitude
reflects the assumption that, notwithstanding its dramatic guise, the
Republic is principally a vehicle for the exposition of Plato's philosophical views, with Socrates as the medium through which those
views are expressed. From this it follows that the serious business
of the dialogue begins only when Socrates engages in recognisably philosophical conversation. The alternative assumption is that
Socrates is not simply Plato's mouthpiece, and that the author's
medium is the dialogue in all its aspects. Consequently, to understand
the *Republic* we must attend to each of these aspects, not least those
of a literary and dramatic nature. On this assumption, it follows that
much might be gleaned from the opening scene, and indeed many
readers consider it to be loaded with prescient detail. An ancient
warrant for doing so is the anecdote related by Dionysius of
Halicarnassus stating that throughout his life Plato repeatedly
revised his writings, and on his death a writing tablet was found
inscribed with different versions of the opening sentence of the
Republic.

For the first-time reader, the significance of the opening scene can
only be assessed retrospectively, since it is only after one has read the
dialogue in its entirety that one can assess whether particular aspects
of the opening scene inform the whole. It is with this in mind that,
before looking at Socrates' exchange with Cephalus, we shall consider
some of the interpretative possibilities on offer.

(a) The Historical Context

For many scholars, the historical context in which the dialogue is set is of paramount significance. There are two points to bear in mind in this regard. First, while it is difficult to determine the precise date of the internal action of the dialogue, we can be confident that it takes place somewhere between 431 BC and 411 BC, specifically in the years preceding the civil conflict that convulsed Athens in the wake of its defeat in 404 BC, and that led to the Spartan-backed regime of the Thirty. Second, while it is also difficult to know precisely when Plato wrote the *Republic*, we know he is writing at a time when the individual fates of the historical characters represented in the dialogue are well known. This is important since many of the characters who inhabit the opening scene were either directly involved in the turmoil of the last decade of the fourth century BC or related to those who were (there are eleven in all, though not all of them speak). Cephalus was a *metic* – a resident foreigner – invited to Athens by the statesman Pericles, presumably because of his expertise in the manufacture of weapons, the source of his significant wealth. His presence in the opening scene is something of an anachronism, since he is thought to have died some time previously. However, the fate of Cephalus' family is of greatest significance. The Thirty executed his son, Polemarchus, on political charges, while another son, Lysias – who does not speak but whose presence is mentioned at 328b – was forced into exile, and the family assets confiscated. According to his own account, Lysias played an important role in the overthrow of the Thirty and the restoration of democracy. Named as one of Polemarchus' companions at 327c, Nicaretus, son of the statesman Nicias – he of the 'Peace' of 421 BC – would also be executed on political charges by the Thirty. In addition to these foreigners and committed democrats, Plato allocates parts to his own brothers, Glaucon and Adeimantus. We know nothing of their particular political affiliations, but we do know that they – and therefore Plato, – were related to Critias and Charmides, both members of the Thirty (Charmides had special responsibility for the Piraeus area). As G. R. F. Ferrari notes, Plato puts his brothers 'on the best of terms with a family whom their kinsmen will ruin' (Ferrari 2000: xii). Lastly, the restored democrats would ultimately execute Socrates, whom we suppose to have been considered dangerous, not least for his association with both Critias and Charmides.

In this context, the location of the conversation is also significant. As the port of Athens, the Piraeus was the point of intersection between Athens and the world beyond, a place where the domestic and the foreign, the established and the new came into contact with one another. Cephalus, as a *metic*, and indeed the goddess Bendis, both foreign and new to Athens, are emblematic in this regard. Consequently, the Piraeus would certainly have been a diverse and even disorderly place, as Aristotle emphasises when reflecting on the potential danger that ports represent to the stability of the cities to which they are attached (see *Politics*, 1327a). Further, the Piraeus was the stronghold of democratic resistance to the Thirty, the phrase 'men of the Piraeus' coming to designate those who fought for democracy. Finally, the decisive battle in the civil conflict, in which Lysias played a leading role and Critias died, took place in front of the temple of Bendis, whose inaugural festival is the pretext for Socrates' visit to the Piraeus.

Readers can make what they will of the historical context, which many commentators emphasise sets the scene for a reading of the *Republic* that emphasises its political content. In Allan Bloom's version, 'the conversation in the *Republic* takes place in the shadow of the Thirty,' and, unless this is borne in mind, 'its teaching cannot be understood' (Bloom 1991: 440). On this view, we cannot ignore that the largely convivial setting in which a disparate group of individuals meet and discuss politics would soon be overwhelmed by political events. Thus conceived, the opening scene emphasises that the fate of individuals cannot be separated from their political situation. To overlook this, it is argued, obscures the central theme of the dialogue.

(b) The Mythological Context

Others emphasise the mythological context of the opening scene. Articulated most comprehensively by Eva Brann, attention focuses on the opening line and the reference to Socrates' descent ('I went down yesterday to the Piraeus . . .'). The imagery of descent and ascent certainly pervades the dialogue as a whole. Most famously, at the centre of the dialogue, we find the ascent from the cave and the philosopher's subsequent return, and at its conclusion the account of a descent and ascent out of the Underworld, Hades, in the 'Myth of Er'. Brann takes this symmetry very seriously, and conceives an elaborate arrangement whereby the beginning of the dialogue is understood as much in mythological terms as the 'myth of Er' with which it ends.

According to Brann, Socrates' descent to the Piraeus is understood as a descent to the 'beyond land', a reference to Hades. The suggestion would have sounded more immediately plausible to Plato's original audience because of an ancient belief that the Piraeus had once been an island separated from the mainland – and thereby Athens – by a river. In the words 'the Piraeus,' Plato's audience would have heard the reference to '*he Peraie*,' meaning 'the beyond land'. So in the opening line, Socrates is saying something like 'I went down yesterday to the land beyond the river'. There he meets Cephalus – who on Brann's account represents Pluto, the god of the Underworld – an elderly man who is said to have 'reached the time of life which the poets call "old age, the threshold"' (328e). In short, Cephalus is at the threshold of death, when he will enter the darkness of Hades. On the subject of darkness, we note further that the opening scene is set at the close of day. 'We are in the city of shades', Brann maintains (Brann 2004: 118).

Conceived in this context, Socrates stands for the god Heracles. The last of Heracles' twelve labours was to descend into Hades and return to the light with the triple-headed monster, Cerberus, which he is instructed to tame by words alone, without the use of force. For Brann, the *Republic* is Socrates' attempt to replicate this ascent, to journey from the darkness of ignorance to the light of knowledge. Significantly, Socrates' third and most formidable interlocutor in Book I, Thrasymachus, represents Cerberus, whose argument concerning justice Socrates has to expose to the light of truth. Following the initial confrontation with Thrasymachus, this task continues to occupy Socrates for the remainder of the dialogue.

Again readers can make of this what they will. While at first glance it might appear rather fanciful, there is much to be said for Brann's reading, though it might be criticised for distracting attention from the political significance of the opening scene. Moreover, those readers who more or less pass by the opening lines might ask how Brann's reconstruction helps us to understand the philosophical content of the dialogue. Against this, one might contend that it provides a coherent contextual schema within which the dialogue as a whole can be viewed. As such, it represents a powerful counter-argument to those who view the *Republic* as a sprawling and ultimately disjointed work.

(c) The Philosophical Context

What I shall term the philosophical context of the opening scene also draws on the notion of descent contained in the first line of the dialogue but in a non-mythological way. In some of its various versions, there is also considerable overlap with the political significance that is imputed to the historical context. I shall nonetheless treat it as a distinct conception of the opening scene, since it draws particular attention to the status and task of the philosopher.

We have observed that the opening scene is rich in dramatic detail and that this serves to locate the discussion in a specific situation. For many readers, the effect of this is to emphasise that philosophical discussion takes place not in a social void, but emerges from everyday situations. For us it may have become a rather abstract and specialised discipline associated with the lecture hall and the academic journal, but in the opening scene of the *Republic*, philosophy is rooted in ordinary experiences such as a trip to see a religious festival and a visit to the home of an old acquaintance.

To understand this, it is argued, has important implications for how we read the opening scene. First, in so far as any philosophical encounter takes place within a particular social milieu, it is essential to grasp how this shapes the manner in which the encounter unfolds. The milieu provides the opportunity for philosophical dialogue, but it also limits it. This applies not only to the immediate physical environment – in the *Republic*, a domestic setting in the Piraeus during a time of relative peace – but also the participants. That said, it is of the nature of philosophical discourse that it is not wholly confined by its milieu. Indeed, it is precisely aimed at transcending that context, to move from the subjective to the objective, from opinion to knowledge, and it is in this relation we are to conceive Socrates' descent. Socrates must descend to the Piraeus, a melting pot of contrasting opinions and perceptions, for it is in disagreement rooted in everyday experience that philosophy begins. Only from such a starting point can Socrates endeavour to ascend, to attempt the progress from opinion to knowledge that constitutes the dialogical task of philosophy. Still it remains a process rooted in the ordinary and imperfect world. The theme of the relation between philosophy and the world, it is suggested, manifests itself in various forms as the dialogue proceeds (the relation between the ideal and the possible, the theoretical and the practical, the physical and the metaphysical, and so on).

This reading overlaps with the historical reading if the point about philosophy emerging from everyday experience is conceived in terms of the relation between philosophy and politics, in particular the exercise of political power. Viewed in this light, many readings dwell on the initial exchange in which Socrates is persuaded to remain in the Piraeus (327c–328b). Socrates confirms it is his intention to return home, and, accompanied by his retinue, Polemarchus asks, 'do you see how many of us there are? . . .You must either get the better of all these people or else stay here'. To this playful threat of force, Socrates suggests an alternative possibility: 'we might persuade you that you should let us go'. Polemarchus replies that this would be unlikely to succeed 'if we refused to listen'. The point is made that this exchange subtly anticipates certain key themes that will develop as the dialogue unfolds. Different interpretations place emphasis on different elements, but central to many is the tension between, on one hand, the philosopher's *logos* – this important Greek word means both 'reason' and 'discourse' – and, on the other, the simple threat of physical force or the will of a majority that refuses to heed the philosopher's words. In short, it raises the question of the relation between the philosopher and the political community of which he is a part.

With these possibilities – or perhaps none of them – in mind, we shall proceed to Socrates' debate with Cephalus.

The Conversation with Cephalus (328b–331d)

The conversation with Cephalus is brief and has the air of small talk, but it raises the central question of the dialogue as a whole: 'what is justice (*dikaiosune*)?'

Greeting him, the aged Cephalus laments that Socrates does not visit more often, since 'the more the pleasures of the body fade, the greater becomes one's desire and taste for conversation' (328d). An innocuous remark perhaps, but it may be viewed as rather patronising. Though Cephalus would not appear to have intended it as such, his words may be said to imply that philosophical reflection is not to be taken too seriously; it has its place – or rather its time, namely old age – but ought not to interfere with the serious business of living one's life. Whether readers accept this interpretation very much depends on whether they view Plato's portrait of Cephalus to be a sympathetic one. Ought we to accept Annas' view that there are 'enough malicious touches in Plato's picture of Cephalus to show us that we are being presented with a limited and complacent man'? (Annas 1981: 19). Or is C. D. C. Reeve right to maintain that Cephalus is 'an attractive character, portrayed with delicacy and respect'? (Reeve 2006: 6). How one decides this matter has significant implications for how the conversation itself is understood.

Socrates presses Cephalus on the topic of old age: 'would you call it a difficult time of life?' he asks (328e). Cephalus replies that, unlike those of his peers who lament the loss of their youth and 'recite a litany of grievances against old age' (329b), he is glad to be rid of youthful desire, and cites the playwright Sophocles as his authority (329b–c). Old age, he concludes, 'is a final release from a bunch of insane masters' (329d). Socrates seems impressed, but suggests that many would attribute Cephalus' equanimity in the face of old age to his considerable wealth (329e). Cephalus concedes the point, while insisting that what truly matters is an individual's temperament: 'the wrong temperament, even with the aid of wealth, will never be at peace with itself' (330a). Socrates probes further: what has been the greatest benefit of possessing wealth? (330d). It is in response to this question that justice is first mentioned. Cephalus says that old age prompts a reassessment of one's life in advance of what might happen in the afterlife. Reflecting on the possible injustices one has committed, the value of a clear conscience is fully appreciated (here Cephalus cites the poet Pindar as his authority). In this respect, wealth is a blessing for those of good character, since in addition to helping an individual resist the temptation to defraud others, it enables him to repay his debts prior to death (330d–331c).

Cephalus is generally conceived as representative of the authority of old age and conventional wisdom. His references to literary figures such as Sophocles and Pindar testify to this, for it was traditional practice to cite poets on moral and other matters in much the same way that religious believers today cite holy texts. The issue is whether it is an unsympathetic portrait of an old man designed to expose the limitations of an uncritical acceptance of inherited views. Taking up Cephalus' reference to justice, Socrates interrogates the implied definition of it as 'truthfulness, and returning anything that you may have received from someone else' (331c). In a move characteristic of his argumentative method, the *elenchus*, Socrates suggests a case in which Cephalus' definition of justice results in its opposite. Imagine one has borrowed a weapon from a friend. What if, Socrates asks, the friend loses his mind and then asks that the weapon be returned? According to the definition, the just action is to return the weapon. Cephalus immediately concedes that it would be unjust to do so, at which point he makes his excuses and the conversation ends (331d).

Thus Cephalus' definition is seen to crumble at the slightest argumentative touch. This is emblematic, Annas argues, of a complacent and un-philosophical conception of the virtuous life that comprises little more than 'a few simple rules or maxims like "don't lie" and "give back what isn't yours"' (Annas 1981: 20). Importantly, Cephalus' conception of justice reduces the virtuous life to certain actions that must be undertaken for one not to be caught out in the afterlife. Notwithstanding Cephalus' earnest references to the person of good character, on his account of justice, the kind of person one is does not matter as long as one's obligations are fulfilled.

Reeve understands the conversation very differently: Cephalus 'may not know what justice is, but his experience of life has given him a kind of wisdom that Plato by no means despises' (Reeve refers forward to 620c–d) (Reeve 2006: 6). On this account, Cephalus is a decent old man who has led a virtuous life, evident in the moderation he displays in remarking that money is important but insufficient to guarantee happiness on its own. He is the embodiment of moderation – a virtue that, as we shall see, is highly esteemed by Socrates – standing somewhere between his grandfather, who made a huge fortune, and his father, who subsequently lost most of it. 'I shall be happy,' Cephalus says, 'if I can leave these boys not less, but a little bit more, than I inherited' (330b). On Reeve's understanding, the fact that the historical Cephalus' fortune would subsequently be confiscated adds a tragic note to this wish; on a reading following Annas, by contrast, the fact of his future loss is symptomatic of the old man's present complacency. Most importantly, on Reeve's account, Cephalus represents a challenge that Socrates' later account of justice must meet. Socrates will suggest that the truly virtuous individual is the philosopher, yet in Cephalus we are presented with an individual who is 'to some degree moderate, just, pious, and wise without having studied philosophy or knowing what the virtues are'. What then is so special about the philosopher? We shall see how Socrates answers this question as the dialogue unfolds. Perhaps, Reeves suggests, it is not his intellectual inadequacy that causes Plato to retire him after such a short part but the fact that, 'already of good character and disposed to virtue', Cephalus has little need for philosophy (Reeve 2006: 7).

The Conversation with Polemarchus (331d–336a)

Cephalus retires from the discussion in good humour, passing the conversational reins to Polemarchus, heir to his father's view of justice as he is to his fortune. At this point the air of small talk disappears, and the conversation becomes increasingly earnest and focused on the matter at hand. Polemarchus reiterates a modified version of his father's argument, and Socrates then proceeds to show that it is fundamentally flawed, at which point we are back where we started. This may not intimidate readers who are acquainted with other Platonic dialogues, but those new to Plato might be forgiven if they flick forward a few pages, fearful that too much more of the dialogue consists in conversations that appear to make little substantive progress. If they see that, superficially at least, the debate with Thrasymachus takes much the same form, and that at the end of it Socrates declares himself no wiser than when he started, then, supposing that they do not give up on the dialogue altogether, they may be sorely tempted to skip Book I and move straight to Book II, which looks much more promising.

Readers are strongly recommended not to take this option, but to remain with Book I for its duration. All scholarly commentators concede that problems are raised and themes announced in Book I to which the discussion returns in due course, and most agree that it is important to understand how they are first articulated. What is more, it may be that Plato intends the reader to feel a certain frustration and even irritation with the manner in which the discussion proceeds in Book I. I suggested earlier that the principal interpretative question arising from Socrates' first conversation concerns whether or not Plato's portrait of Cephalus is a sympathetic one. In the discussion with Polemarchus, it is Socrates' role that becomes the focus of critical attention. Most commentators agree that the portrait of the son is of an unreflective and complacent individual who only accepts his father's conception of justice because he is a slave to convention. The question is whether Socrates' arguments are substantial, or whether it is simply Polemarchus' philosophical inexperience that enables Socrates to prevail. If it is the latter, then Plato might be making an important point about the limitations of Socrates' argumentative method both in this discussion and in Book I as a whole.

Polemarchus leaps to his father's defence on the authority of the poet Simonides' claim that 'it is just to pay everyone what is owed to him' (331e). Again we note the appeal to a literary figure; although it is not explicitly addressed at this stage, in due course Socrates will have much to say about the moral and epistemological value of literature. Socrates claims not to understand the meaning of Simonides' claim, and obliges Polemarchus to interpret it. In so doing it becomes clear that Polemarchus' aim is to provide a definition that does not fall foul of the sort of counter-examples that undermined his father's argument. The matter turns on what is meant by 'owed'. 'What he [Simonides] thinks is due to friends,' Polemarchus clarifies, 'is to do them good, not harm' (332a), and Socrates' criticism of Cephalus is thereby taken into account: one is not doing a friend good by returning a knife when they have lost their mind. Likewise, Polemarchus adds that enemies should also receive what is due to them, namely 'something harmful' (332b). Thus, Polemarchus' initial definition is that justice involves giving everyone their due: good in the case of a friend, and harm in the case of an enemy.

Socrates offers four counter-arguments. In the first, he argues that, on Polemarchus' definition, justice is largely superfluous (332c–333e). Socrates draws an analogy that was a commonplace of Greek ethical discourse, between the practice of justice and the practice of a skill (*techne*) such as medicine. Each skill, Socrates suggests, is practised in a particular area of human activity: medicine 'gives the body drugs and food and drink', while cookery 'gives flavour to cooked food' (332c–d). On Polemarchus' definition, the skill of justice applies in the area of helping one's friends and harming one's enemies, but Socrates has his doubts. In questions of health, the doctor is best able to help the friend and harm the enemy. Similarly, the ship's captain is best placed to help and to harm at sea. By stages, Polemarchus retreats to the position that justice is of use in 'partnerships involving money' (333b). But here too, Socrates insists, the practice of justice is redundant, since in any specific area of business activity in which one wishes to put money to some use – buying or selling horses, for example – one who knows about horses will be a more useful partner than the just man (333b–c). Justice, it transpires, is only useful when one wishes to keep one's money safe. In Socrates' words, 'it is only when money is useless that justice is useful for dealing with it' (333c–d). This applies to other cases: justice is useful when one wishes a pruning knife to be kept safe, but as soon as one wishes to use it, 'the art of viticulture is what you want' (333d). Justice is only of use 'when things are useless' (333e).

Socrates immediately launches into a further argument based on the skill analogy (333e–334b). Here Polemarchus is led to the conclusion that his just man is 'a kind of thief' (334a). In the same way that the doctor who is skilled at warding off disease is similarly best able to make one ill, so the best guard will also be the most accomplished thief. On the skill analogy it follows that 'if the just man is clever at looking after money, he is also clever at stealing it' (334a). Consequently, in Polemarchus' account, justice turns out to be 'a kind of skill of stealing – but with a view to helping one's friends and harming one's enemies' (334b).

Polemarchus is confused and clearly incapable of mounting a sustained defence: 'I don't any longer know what I was saying,' he concedes (334b). Yet what of the arguments that reduce him to this state of perplexity? Much depends on the reader's attitude to the skill analogy. For Annas, its introduction is justified on the grounds that it enables Socrates to highlight the central weaknesses of Polemarchus' position, most notably the belief that justice consists in actions based on rules such as giving each person their due. With the introduction of the skill analogy, Annas argues, Socrates reveals that he is 'implicitly thinking of these like the rules of a skill, a means of achieving an antecedently determined end' in the way that medicine pursues the end of health. Thus understood, Socrates shows that the end of justice is a trivial one, useful only 'when things are useless'. Likewise, in the second argument the skill analogy enables Socrates to argue that Polemarchus' definition lacks any notion that 'a just action must be aimed at some good'. Instead, as a capacity for opposites, it is seen to support the idea that justice can be used for both good and bad ends (Annas 1981: 26–8).

Reeve, by contrast, follows a number of commentators in adopting a more critical approach to Socrates' introduction of the skill analogy. Reeve concedes that Socrates' first argument highlights the deficiencies in Polemarchus' definition, but suggests that Plato also wishes to direct the reader to Socrates' own deficiencies. Plato does this in the course of Socrates' second argument by highlighting what for Reeve is the most significant flaw in the skill analogy, namely that while a skill such as medicine is a capacity for opposites, the excellence or virtue (*arete*) of justice aims only at what is good. So while, on Annas' reading, this flaw is implicit in Polemarchus' definition, and by the adoption of the skill analogy Socrates draws it out, on Reeve's account, it is principally a flaw in the analogy itself, and one that should lead us to scrutinise Socrates' own procedure. 'Without showing the least awareness of the effect that he might be having on Polemarchus,' Reeve maintains, 'Socrates is casually . . . sowing the seeds of scepticism about traditional values without providing a viable alternative to them' (Reeve 2006: 8). We shall return to possible explanations of Plato's decision to portray Socrates' argumentative practice in a negative light in due course.

Socrates' third argument (334c–335b) follows Polemarchus' stated determination to maintain the definition of justice as 'treating your friends well and your enemies badly' (334b). Socrates asks whether Polemarchus means by friends those whom an individual 'believes to be good, or those who really are good, even if he does not realise it,' and likewise with enemies (334c). Those whom one believes to be good, Polemarchus replies, conceding that mistakes are possible. However, this creates a further problem for Polemarchus' definition, Socrates argues, since if a mistake is made and a man is thought to be bad when in truth he is good, then Polemarchus is committed to the position that it is 'just to harm those who do no wrong' (334d).

Taken aback by Socrates' latest assault, Polemarchus modifies his definition in advance of Socrates' final criticism (335b–336b). 'If someone seems to be good and is, let's call him a friend . . . and let the same definition apply to an enemy', he says (335a). By this altered conception, justice is helping a friend if he is good and harming an enemy if he is bad (335a). But Socrates remains unsatisfied: 'is it really in the nature of a just man to treat anyone in the world badly?' (335b). Polemarchus concedes that to cause anything harm is to make it worse, depriving it of the quality that makes it good; in the case of humans, the excellence of justice. 'In which case, my friend, members of the human race who are treated badly must necessarily become more unjust' (335c). Yet the consequence is that justice acts to produce injustice. Once again, the skill analogy is invoked: 'are musicians able, by means of music, to make people unmusical?' (335c). Impossible, Polemarchus agrees, from which it follows that an individual is incapable of making others unjust in the practice of justice: 'it is not the property of the just man to treat his friend or anyone else badly. It is the property of his opposite, the unjust man' (335d).

Polemarchus capitulates, though like his father he is unperturbed by defeat, and agrees to join Socrates in the 'battle' against anyone who seeks to dispute the conclusion that the just individual harms no one (335e). This constitutes a reverse on Polemarchus' part of which he seems characteristically unaware. Having begun by advancing the most conventional of views regarding justice, he is now proposing to defend a view that would have seemed as radical to Plato's original audience as to those who heard something similar in Christ's Sermon on the Mount. But is Socrates worthy of his victory? The third argument would seem to be the most reputable of them all, the fourth perhaps the least so. Regardless of whether one agrees with Socrates' conclusion, the path by which it is reached is questionable. R. C. Cross and A. D. Woosley argue that Socrates exploits an ambiguity in the word translated as 'harm' (*blaptein*). When Polemarchus speaks of harming enemies, he means harming their interests rather than making them worse men. But Socrates trades on the latter meaning of 'harm' in his final argument, unchallenged by the inexperienced Polemarchus (Cross and Woosley 1964: 20–2). Annas questions this criticism while adding her own, describing as 'breath-taking' Socrates' unsupported assumption that justice is the human excellence – what it takes to be a good specimen of humanity – in the same way that we might speak of a good specimen of a horse or a dog (Annas 1981: 33). Again Polemarchus fails to notice any problem, but the moot point is whether Plato intends the reader to notice Socrates' abuses of the younger man's philosophical shortcomings. However, since Socrates' final confrontation raises the same issue, we shall only examine it once we have considered Thrasymachus' contribution to the evening.

The Conversation with Thrasymachus (336b–354b)

If to this point the discussion has largely proceeded on amicable terms, then with Thrasymachus' entry the atmosphere changes altogether. Cheered on, perhaps, by readers frustrated by the preceding conversation, Thrasymachus – his name means something like 'wild fighter' – tears into Socrates for the manner in which the debate has been conducted.

Another non-Athenian among the assembled company, Thrasymachus of Chalcedon is a historical figure known to us from sources besides Plato. A sophist specialising in the teaching and practice of rhetoric, Thrasymachus was clearly an important intellectual figure, though we do not know whether he held the views that Plato ascribes to him. In the *Republic*, the discussion begins as though Socrates and Thrasymachus are old rivals between whom little love is lost. Socrates suggests that he noticed Thrasymachus becoming increasingly agitated during the discussion with Polemarchus but was still shocked by his aggressive intervention: 'he gathered himself and sprang at us, like a wild beast at its prey' (336b).

Thrasymachus takes Socrates to task for not proposing his own definition of justice, instead 'asking questions, and scoring points by proving that any answer given by anyone is wrong' (336c). Thrasymachus would seem to have a point, though he then adds irritably: 'don't go telling us that it's what's necessary, or what's beneficial, or what's advantageous, or what's profitable, or what's good for you. I won't take any of that stuff' (336d). Socrates' response appears designed to exasperate Thrasymachus further. Do not chastise us unduly, he begs, 'we lack the ability. So when you clever people see our efforts, pity is really a far more appropriate reaction than annoyance' (336–337a). Thrasymachus continues to complain about Socrates, who replies that it is difficult to answer when Thrasymachus has already closed off most of the possible responses (337a–b). They continue to exchange verbal blows, Socrates pleading that he cannot define what he does not know, and suggesting that it makes much more sense for Thrasymachus to present his own definition

(337e–338a). The latter agrees to do so, but the debate commences in a very bad humour indeed, with Thrasymachus confirmed in his suspicion that Socrates will never be drawn into stating his own position, and Socrates adding in an aside that Thrasymachus was looking for and excuse to state his own view all along (338a–b).

The discussion is not always easy to follow due to the difficulty of establishing the precise nature of either Thrasymachus' position or Socrates' criticisms of it. I shall begin by clarifying Thrasymachus' account of justice before considering the extent to which Socrates successfully refutes it. Commentators contest the latter whilst for the most part agreeing that the confrontation has an important bearing on what follows, specifying the intellectual challenge that Socrates has to meet in the remainder of the dialogue.

(a) Thyrasymachus' Conception of Justice (338c–344c)

Thrasymachus declares that 'justice is simply what is good for the stronger' (338c). By 'the stronger' he means 'the ruling power' in a given jurisdiction, regardless of its constitutional character: 'in all cities the same thing is just, namely, what is good for the ruling authority' (338d–339e). Characterised in this way, Thrasymachus' definition might be said to represent another popular view of justice, this one advanced by Athenians of a more sceptical – or perhaps cynical – persuasion. It certainly alters the terms of the debate. Up to this point Socrates has set his sights on an abstract definition of justice that transcends particular instances of it. By contrast, Thrasymachus offers a sociological account of justice as simply that which is prescribed by the law. If, in one jurisdiction, the ruling power deems it lawful for humans to eat animals, then it is just. If, in another, it is deemed unlawful, then in that jurisdiction it is unjust. Justice is a sociological issue concerning the exercise of political power.

In his initial response, Socrates persists in viewing the definition in philosophical rather than sociological terms, making the point that, in spite of Thrasymachus' strictures about permissible answers, they both agree that justice is 'something that is good for a person'. The disagreement is over Thrasymachus' addition of good 'for the stronger' (339a–b). In addition, Socrates attempts to shift the focus of debate from the rulers to the ruled by drawing attention to the point that, on Thrasymachus' account, it is 'just for subjects to obey their rulers' (339b). Thrasymachus assents to this and to the next question concerning the possibility that rulers make mistakes (339c). The second concession enables Socrates to establish that in a situation where a law is enforced which is contrary to the rulers' interest, it is not only just for the ruled 'to do what is good for the stronger, but also its opposite, what is not good for him' (339c). Thrasymachus looks for clarification. The problem, Socrates reiterates, is that in the case of rulers miscalculating their interests, 'the weaker have been ordered to do what is *not* good for the stronger' (339e).

Cleitophon now makes his solitary intervention in the dialogue, challenging Socrates' conclusion (340a). Cleitophon suggests that by 'good for the stronger' Thrasymachus 'meant what the stronger *thought* was good for him' (340b). If this were accepted by Thrasymachus, then it would remove the crucial premise of Socrates' preceding argument – that rulers might mistakenly prescribe what is not in their interest – by identifying justice with what the ruler believes to be his interest rather than what truly is in his interest. Further, it would reiterate the sociological nature of Thrasymachus' account. But Thrasymachus dismisses Cleitophon's suggestion, choosing instead to reject Socrates' premise by revising what he means by 'ruler': 'do you imagine I regard a person who makes a mistake, at the moment when he is making the mistake, as stronger?' he asks (340c). A true ruler is an expert, like a doctor or an accountant, and no expert 'to the extent that he *is* what we call him, ever makes a mistake' (340e). A ruler, then, is not a ruler in the strict sense when he makes an error, since at the point that knowledge of the skill of ruling fails him, he ceases to be a ruler.

Thrasymachus believes that this correction enables him to retain his conception of justice intact: since a true ruler does not make mistakes, 'he *does* enact what is best for him, and this is what his subject must carry out. So as I said originally, my definition is that it is just to do what is good for the stronger' (341a). However, in reintroducing the skill analogy, Thrasymachus departs from his initial sociological account. Justice is no longer conceived in relativist terms as whatever a given power determines it to be. Instead, it is absorbed into an idealist account of the 'ruler in the most precise sense possible' (341b). In other words, Thrasymachus shifts from an account of how rulers *do* behave to an account of how they *ought* to behave – namely, in their own interest.

Thrasymachus' revised position becomes clearer as Socrates proceeds to challenge it. Socrates takes up the reintroduction of the skill analogy, and challenges the claim that ruling is a skill that serves the interest of the ruler himself (341c–342e). For as the doctor pursues the interest of his patient in the practice of medicine, and the ship's captain pursues the interest of his crew in the practice of navigation, so the practice of ruling is not to the benefit of the true ruler but of his subjects: 'no one in a position of authority, to the extent that he *is* in authority,' Socrates argues, 'thinks about or prescribes what is good for himself, but only what is good for the person or thing under his authority' (342e). This would appear to turn Thrasymachus' position on its head, he adds. The true ruler, it seems, exercises his power in the interest not of himself but of others (343a).

A long speech follows in which Thrasymachus attempts to meet Socrates' argument with the counter-example of the shepherd, as popular a metaphor for the ruler in ancient Greek literature as it is in the Bible. Thrasymachus contends that as shepherds only think of their own interest in practising animal husbandry – shepherds do not fatten their flock for the benefit of the sheep themselves – so true rulers 'regard their subjects as their sheep' (343b). Subjects exist in order to provide for the happiness (*eudaimonia*) of the ruler. Warming to his theme, Thrasymachus confirms his transition from sociologist to apologist for tyranny by condemning as nonsense the claim that obeying justice enables a human to flourish: 'you can't avoid the conclusion . . . that a just man comes off worse than an unjust man in every situation' (343d). That injustice is the key to human happiness is exemplified by the lives of tyrants: 'they are called blessed and happy' by all who hear of their exploits, Thrasymachus maintains. 'Those who condemn injustice do so not through fear of practising it, but through fear of experiencing it' (344b–c). With this Thrasymachus' immoralism becomes clear: justice is for the weak and inhibited, while injustice is a manifestation of strength, freedom and power.

(b) Socrates' Response to Thrasymachus (344d–354c)
Conceived as a sociological account of justice, it was observed that Thrasymachus' original intervention would have altered the terms of the debate significantly had Socrates allowed it to in his initial response. Socrates does not resist a different alteration occasioned by

Thrasymachus' statement of immoralism. Rather than the definition of justice, the debate now focuses on the question of whether 'injustice is something more profitable than justice' (345a). However, Socrates relates that it looked initially as though no further argument would take place at all. Having concluded his speech, Thrasymachus prepared to depart but was prevailed upon by those assembled to justify himself. Socrates says given the gravity of the topic, he too was insistent: 'we are trying to define the whole conduct of life – how each of us can live his life in the most profitable way' (344e).

Socrates recommences by rejecting the shepherd as a counter-example to the claim that skills are practised in the interests of others: 'the skill of being a shepherd . . . is surely not concerned with anything other than making the best provision for what is under its direction' (345d). At 345e–347d, Socrates argues that if the shepherd benefits himself, then it is because in addition to animal husbandry, he practises a second skill, 'the art of earning a living' (346b). The same applies to all skilled practitioners. In earning a living, one skill is practised, but this is distinct from the practice of the skill for which they are paid. However it is viewed, this is a strange argument. Having previously argued that the practitioner of any skill acts not in his own interest but in the interest of others, Socrates now cites an example of a skill – earning a living – that only benefits the practitioner. As Reeve observes, 'Socrates' second argument itself undermines his first' (Reeve 2006: 19). The argument might nevertheless be said to contain an important point. While Socrates is wrong to insist there are two separate skills involved when a shepherd practises animal husbandry for payment, it is true that, in Sean Sayers' words, there are 'two distinguishable *aspects*' to the practice of the shepherd's skill (Sayers 1999: 14). The same applies to the true ruler. As such, the true ruler works for the benefit of those whom he rules, and not for payment. Following a request for clarification from Glaucon (347a), Socrates suggests that true rulers do not seek any financial reward. Their payment is not being 'ruled by someone worse', and it is 'this fear which makes decent people rule' (347c). 'If there were ever a city of good men,' he adds, 'there would probably be as much competition *not* to rule as there is among us to rule' (347d). There will be cause to recall this observation later in the dialogue.

Socrates' next argument focuses on Thrasymachus' claim that injustice is more profitable than justice (348b–350d). It follows Thrasymachus' refusal to concede that justice is a human excellence and comprises what is generally considered the weakest of Socrates' arguments in Book I. Socrates argues that, unlike justice, injustice cannot be a human excellence because it is not a skill: 'do you think that one just man would be at all prepared to try and outdo another just man?' he asks (349b). Thrasymachus agrees that while just men do not attempt to outdo one another, unjust men are constantly locked in competition. Indeed, Thrasymachus adds, the unjust man – as exemplified by the tyrant – 'thinks it right to outdo *everyone*' in an effort to seize all that he can for himself (349c). As such the unjust man is 'wise and good', the opposite of the just man (349d). Drawing on the examples of the skilled and unskilled musician and doctor, Socrates argues that the skilled practitioner never attempts to outdo other skilled practitioners. For example, skilled musicians do not seek to outdo one another when tuning a lyre, instead they seek to accomplish the same end in accordance with the dictates of their skill.

Thrasymachus concedes the point when he might have replied that while just men might not attempt to 'outdo' in the sense of cheating one another, they certainly attempt to 'outdo' one another in honest competition (the term 'outdo' translates the Greek term *pleonexia*, which contains both of these senses, and the argument trades on this ambiguity). Musicians may not engage in competitive tuning, but they do strive to outdo their peers as performers. In addition, Thrasymachus might have observed that the truly unjust man is identical to the skilled musician in that neither attempts to exceed the principles of their respective skills; like the musician in the practice of his skill, the truly unjust man seeks to practise injustice as completely as possible. The failure to make either point is fatal to Thrasymachus' case. Indeed, the faults in the argument are so glaring that it begs the question of whether Plato himself was aware of them. If he is, then we might again wonder whether Plato intends to draw our attention to Thrasymachus' lack of philosophical acumen and/or the limitations of Socrates' own approach. This aside, having also agreed that the skilled musician is knowledgeable and good while the unskilled musician is ignorant and bad, Socrates is able to match the non-competitive just individual with the skilled musician, and the competitive unjust individual with the unskilled musician: as the just man 'is like the wise and good man', so 'the unjust man is like the bad and ignorant' (350c). Socrates dwells on Thrasymachus' increasing discomfort: 'I saw something I had never seen before,' he relates, 'Thrasymachus blushing' (350d).

Socrates' penultimate argument focuses on Thrasymachus' claim at 344c that injustice is 'stronger, more free and more powerful' than justice (351a–352d). Socrates now dispenses with the skill analogy and proceeds in terms of the difference between the just and the unjust city (*polis*). He asks whether in any joint venture aiming at injustice, be it political, military or criminal, those involved will succeed if they treat one another unjustly. Socrates' point is that injustice 'produces faction and hatred . . . whereas justice produces co-operation and friendship' (351d), for if so, then no city can flourish if its citizens treat one another unjustly. Socrates concludes by extending the argument to the citizens themselves: injustice, he suggests, will render the individual 'incapable of action, because he is at odds with himself' (352a).

Like its predecessor, this argument does not survive too much analysis, though the parallel Socrates suggests between the structure of the city and the individuals that comprise it will be hugely significant later in the discussion. As it appears in this argument, however, the parallel is wholly unsubstantiated. Reeve observes that it is unclear why an unjust group might not treat one another justly but together pursue injustice (Reeve 2006: 20). In addition, Annas makes the point that, in order to gain the co-operation of others, the tyrant needs only 'to pretend to be just' (Annas 1981: 53).

Socrates immediately embarks on his final argument with an indifferent Thrasymachus offering hollow assent (352d–354a). It is unique in seeking to establish a positive case for justice as the means to human happiness. Socrates begins by establishing the premise that the function or work (*ergon*) of an object is an activity it alone does or it does more perfectly than anything else, and the excellence of an object is what enables it to fulfil its function. Thus, the function of the eye is to see, while its excellence is the power of sight that enables it to do so. Socrates then asks Thrasymachus to identify the function of the human soul (*psuche*). Thrasymachus agrees that the function of the soul is 'living' (353d), and, with reference to an earlier though unspecified point of agreement, that its excellence is justice, the practice of the latter enabling the individual soul to flourish (350e). This allows Socrates to conclude that the 'just soul and the just man will have a good life', flourishing in the fulfilment of function, 'and the unjust man, a bad one'. In short, he insists, the argument shows that 'injustice . . . is never more profitable than justice' (353e–354a).

As we shall see, the significance of Socrates' argument lies in the suggested link between human flourishing and the fulfilment of function. However, in its present incarnation it begs a number of questions. We might wonder precisely what Socrates means by 'soul'. Socrates' conclusion refers to the 'just soul *and* the just man', while the premise on which this conclusion depends – namely that the virtue of the soul is justice – specifies the soul alone. Is a human being simply its soul? Or is it soul plus body? We might also query what Socrates means by the 'function' of the soul, and question whether the human soul possesses a function in the manner of the eye and the ear. It is often observed in this connection that function refers not to the specifiable purpose of an object in the way that we might speak of the purpose of a toaster, merely to its characteristic activity. On that basis, we might well concede that living a human life is indeed the characteristic activity of humans. The principal problem is the claim that justice is the excellence enabling the human soul to fulfil its function of living, which Socrates claims to have established elsewhere. Yet it is difficult to determine the point in the discussion to which he refers. Ferrari directs the reader to 350c–d, but even supposing that he has established justice as *a* human excellence, the current argument relies on him having established that it is *the* human excellence (Ferrari 2000: 33).

Still Socrates has emerged victorious, and Thrasymachus invites him to make the most of it (354a). The offer is rejected. There is no cause for celebration, Socrates insists, since they failed to arrive at a definition of justice. Instead they have allowed themselves to become distracted by questions relating to the attributes of justice, first of all 'whether it's wickedness and ignorance, or wisdom and goodness,' and subsequently the claim that 'injustice was more profitable than justice'. Crucially, they have considered whether y is a property of x without having first ascertained the precise nature of x. As a result, Socrates ends, 'I am none the wiser' (354c).

What is the Point of Book I?

The reader might be forgiven for finding the conclusion to Book I to be something of an anti-climax. It is also understandable if the reader is initially unappeased by the promise that all will become clear when the questions raised in Book I are answered in Books II–X. As Socrates himself concedes, little or no tangible progress has been made. Worse still, Socrates says this believing that his arguments have been successful, when the reader's attention has been drawn to their potential deficiencies. The question is whether the argument from deferred gratification is all that might be offered to the reader who has arrived at the end of Book I somewhat disgruntled. For while White considers Book I to be little more than a 'prologue' to the main feature (White 1979: 61), other commentators offer more expansive accounts of its significance.

One alternative develops a suggestion made earlier in relation to Plato's adoption of the dialogue form. Allusion was made there to Christopher Rowe's argument that Plato understood the distance between the philosophical discourse he attempts to instantiate in the dialogues and the conventional types of discourse to which his audience would have been accustomed. Consequently, the dialogues take their points of departure from conventional points of view in an effort to show that their basic assumptions are inadequate, thereby drawing the audience over to Plato's perspective in anticipation of a properly philosophical discourse. Book I of the *Republic* might be considered a case in point. In Rowe's words, Plato 'is perpetually moving, and trying to mediate between, his own (Socratic) perspective and that of his audience', the latter represented in the dialogue by the conventional views of justice professed by Cephalus, Polemarchus and Thrasymachus. In reading Book I, Rowe contends, we must not forget that Plato is attempting to persuade the reader as Socrates attempts to persuade his own interlocutors. 'There is undoubtedly a rhetorical aspect to his writing,' Rowe suggests, 'insofar as it is designed specifically to address an audience of a certain kind' (Rowe 2006: 17).

The implicit assumption of Rowe's approach is that the views expressed by Socrates in Book I are consistent with those expressed by Socrates in Books II–X. This is not the case in respect of a separate rationale for Book I, which insists on a disjunction between it and the later books. The argument takes different forms, but most are based on the speculation that Book I was originally a dialogue written early in Plato's career that the author subsequently revised and re-utilised as the introduction to the *Republic*. There is circumstantial evidence to support this thesis, since Book I differs markedly from those that follow, not least on stylistic grounds. Furthermore, Book I is rich in dramatic detail. As we have seen, the reader is made well aware of the context in which the discussion takes place, and the participants are vividly drawn and have much to say. This stands in marked contrast to Books II–X, where the dramatic context is less evident and only two characters contribute besides Socrates (and even then, it might be argued, their function is largely to prevent the dialogue from becoming a monologue). In addition, Book I is similar in structure to what are traditionally considered Plato's early 'Socratic' dialogues, in which Socrates interrogates the views of others on a given topic without providing an alternative account of his own. Having said that, other commentators insist that the thematic continuities between Book I and what follows are too extensive for Book I to have been a completely separate dialogue, preferring instead the hypothesis that Plato wrote Book I in imitation of his earlier style. Nonetheless, the central point remains: Plato intended Book I to contrast with Books II–X. The question is why he should wish to do this.

Again different answers abound, though all draw attention to the shortcomings in Socrates' arguments, especially those in response to Thrasymachus. In Annas' version it is significant that, while Thrasymachus loses the argument, he is not convinced of his error (see 350d–e). For Annas, Book I highlights the 'ineffectiveness of Socratic methods in dealing with the powerful claim of the moral sceptic' who disagrees with Socrates in a 'basic and systematic way'. Book II represents a fresh start in which the arguments Socrates failed to substantiate in Book I are re-articulated in a broader discussion that appeals to the 'philosophical imagination as well as to the narrower kind of cleverness' tested by the *elenchus* (Annas 1981: 57). Significantly, on Annas's account the failure of Book I is as much a reflection of Thrasymachus' failings as it is of Socrates' own limitations.

Other answers set greater store by Socrates' part in the failure to make substantive progress in Book I. Thus, Reeve argues that Book I is a 'brilliant critique' of the *elenchus* – specifically as it is associated with the historical Socrates – 'every aspect of which is designed to reveal a flaw in his theories'. Plato carries out this exposé in advance of making a fresh start in Book II precisely to show that such a fresh start is required. For Reeve, Plato stages Socrates' failure in Book I with a view to making a new start on his own 'Platonic' terms in Book II. In other words, he bids goodbye to his mentor's methods, while continuing to honour his legacy by retaining him as the principal speaker (Reeve 2006: 23). On this account, it is little wonder that some readers are dissatisfied with Socrates in Book I; it is part of Plato's plan all along.

Books II–V (357a–471c)

We now turn to Books II-V, beginning with the restatement of the argument against justice by Glaucon and Adeimantus (357a–367e), continuing with Socrates' defence of justice in terms of the city-soul analogy (367e–445e), and concluding with a consideration of the role of women and the family (449a–471c). The discussion gives the lie to Thrasymachus' accusation at 337a that Socrates asks but never answers his own questions, and contains many of the ideas for which the *Republic* is best known, raising a host of interpretative issues to which the attentive reader must attend.

Beginning Again: Socrates' Task (357a–367e)

Book II opens with a restatement of the problem of justice that clarifies Socrates' task in what follows. Glaucon is first to speak, and his words are then supplemented by Adeimantus. As we have already observed, Glaucon and Adeimantus are at least nominally based on historical figures: they were Plato's brothers, though we do not know what bearing their real personae had on the respective roles they assume in the *Republic*. Whatever additional importance commentators attach to their stepping centre stage at this point, all agree that it significantly alters the relationship between the interlocutors. The confrontational atmosphere of Book I is transformed. Glaucon and Adeimantus look to Socrates for enlightenment, and this allows Socrates the freedom to engage in lengthy exposition. Nonetheless, they prove to be forthright and demanding pupils, not least in their initial restatement of the argument.

(a) Glaucon's Classification of Goods (357a–358b)

As Glaucon instigated Socrates' accession to Polemarchus' request at the beginning of the dialogue, so it is Glaucon who insists that the discussion does not end with the besting of Thrasymachus. He issues a robust challenge Socrates cannot refuse without imitating Thrasymachus' true ruler: 'do you *really* want to convince us that it is in every way better to be just than unjust,' Glaucon asks, 'or is it enough merely to *seem* to have convinced us?' (357b). Clearly, Glaucon is as unconvinced by Socrates' arguments as the attentive reader (an indication, perhaps, that Plato is aware of their shortcomings). To emphasise the point, Glaucon compares Socrates to a 'snake-charmer' by whom Thrasymachus was too easily 'bewitched' (358b).

Glaucon specifies Socrates' task by distinguishing three ways of understanding the good of an object. The first is 'a good of the kind we would choose to have because we value it for its own sake, and not from any desire for its results' (357b). Glaucon offers the example of enjoyment and harmless pleasures, intrinsic goods valued not for what they lead to but as ends. The second is 'the sort we value both for itself and for its consequences'. The examples offered are the ability to think and see, and good health (357c). The supposition is that we value such goods both for their own sakes and for what they result in, enabling us to undertake activities that would otherwise be beyond us. The third type of good includes activities such as physical exercise, submitting to medical treatment and working for a living. These we value not 'for their own sakes, but only for the . . . benefits which result from them' (357c–d). Each is an instrumental good, beneficial not as an end but as the means to an end.

Socrates is asked to locate justice within this threefold classification. He places it in the second class, 'valued by anyone who wants to be happy, both for itself and for its consequences' (358a). Glaucon asks Socrates to substantiate this with an account of 'what each of them [justice and injustice] is, and what effect it has, just by itself, when it is present in the soul. I want to forget about the rewards and results it brings' (358b).

There is considerable dispute over the precise character of the challenge that Socrates is set in this exchange. The issue has significant long-term implications for how the reader judges the success of Socrates' response, but it is of immediate concern to the reader who wishes to understand the normative character of the debate. In modern ethical discourse, a distinction is commonly made between deontological and teleological approaches. According to the deontologist, moral value is intrinsic: an action is just irrespective of its consequences. Thus, according to Immanuel Kant, for example, the moral imperative to tell the truth is categorical and admits of no exceptions based on a calculation of the consequences of lying or not lying in a given set of circumstances. By contrast, the teleologist understands moral value to be instrumental: an action is just and right based on a calculation of its consequences. The utilitarianism of Jeremy Bentham and J. S. Mill epitomises this approach. For the utilitarian, there is no categorical imperative to tell the truth in all circumstances; whether it is right to lie in a given set of circumstances depends on a calculation of which action will contribute most to the happiness of those touched by it.

Let us agree that Socrates' response to Glaucon ascribes both intrinsic and instrumental value to justice, and that in reply Glaucon tells him to set the latter value aside and to focus on the former. The critical question is whether this sets Socrates a challenge that is most accurately characterised as deontological or teleological.

At first glance, it might be thought that Glaucon requests an account of the deontological value of justice. Socrates and Glaucon already agree that justice is wanted for its consequences; for example, it enables one to secure a good reputation. Thus, Socrates understands that an account of the intrinsic value of justice is required. However, if this were indeed the case, one might counter, then one would expect Socrates to have named justice among the first class of goods, valued not as means but as ends. Instead, he places it in the second class, 'valued . . . both for itself and for its consequences'. Yet, in its turn this casts doubt over whether we can characterise Socrates' task in teleological – and in particular utilitarian – terms, for then we might expect him to have named justice among the third class of goods, valued 'only for the . . . benefits which result from them'. Perhaps the problem is the identification of a teleological account with utilitarianism alone, for a third possibility is suggested by Glaucon's interest in justice 'when it is present in the soul'. This would confirm a shift that has already taken place in the distance travelled between Cephalus' definition of justice as a property of actions, and Socrates' concluding argument that justice is a property of the soul. Perhaps the discussion will resist categorisation in Kantian or utilitarian terms, because its focus is the just agent rather than the just action. This would instead identify the discourse in the *Republic* as a species of what is commonly termed 'virtue ethics': fundamentally teleological in its concern with human fulfilment, as Socrates clearly is, but not straightforwardly utilitarian in as much as he does not believe moral value to be wholly determined by an assessment of an action's consequences. On this conception of Socrates' task, Glaucon is seeking an alternative to Thrasymachus' ideal tyrant.

(b) Restating the Case for Injustice (358b–367e)

Playing devil's advocate, Glaucon revives Thrasymachus' argument to provide Socrates with a specific account to oppose. Glaucon's restatement falls into three parts.

In the first part, Glaucon invokes a distinction commonly made in contemporary ethical debate between nature (*phusis*) and convention (*nomos*) (358e–359b). The origin of justice is found not in nature, he says, but in a convention adopted by humans as a compromise. Glaucon anticipates the social contract theory of Thomas Hobbes to a significant extent (see Hobbes 1996). Humans are naturally inclined to do wrong at the expense of others if it will benefit them, and to avoid being on the receiving end of others doing the same. But having tasted both, they come to see that it will benefit them if they arrive at a compromise with one another 'not to do wrong and not to be wronged' (359a). An agreement is reached, and the conventions that are laid down define justice. No sane person would submit to such an agreement if they thought that they could commit wrong without suffering wrong at the hands of others. Hence, justice 'finds its value merely in people's want of power to do wrong' (359b).

This conclusion leads into the second part of Glaucon's restatement in which he argues that justice is the refuge of the weak (359b–360d). Give any 'just' human being sufficient power, and 'led on by greed and the desire to outdo others, he would follow the same course the unjust man follows'. Glaucon illustrates the point with the story of Gyges. A lowly shepherd comes into possession of a ring that enables him to become invisible to others. He visits the king to report on the flocks, and uses the ring to seduce the king's wife, kill the king, and seize power. Were there two such rings, and one were given to a just and the other to an unjust individual, since the ring bestows power without fear of detection, the just as much as the unjust individual would, like the shepherd, quickly succumb to temptation. 'No one is just voluntarily, but only under compulsion,' Glaucon concludes. Only the simple-minded disagree that injustice is more profitable than justice (360c).

In the final part of the argument, Glaucon contends that justice is only beneficial for the social advantages that accrue from possessing a *reputation* for justice (360e–362c). He contrasts the unjust individual who appears to be a paragon of justice with the just individual who acquires an unwarranted reputation for injustice (360e–361b). Glaucon sketches a scenario in which all manner of suffering is visited on the just individual, while the unjust individual receives every social advantage available. Only at the point of an excruciating death does the persecuted individual understand the moral of the story: it is better to emulate the unjust individual, since 'the important thing to aim for is not *being* just, but *appearing* to be just' (362a).

Adeimantus' contribution lacks the focus of his brother's efforts while covering much the same ground. Adeimantus considers the defence of justice commonly offered to sons by their fathers: be just, or at least appear to be just, and all the benefits to be had in this life and the next will be yours (362d–367e). Even the gods can be placated with offerings and sacrifices, assuming that they exist and that they care about human affairs in the first place. Young people are bombarded with the same cynical attitude to justice from every side, Adeimantus asserts. Is it any wonder that few are 'prepared to respect justice, rather than laugh when they hear it being recommended?' (366c). What is needed is a defence of justice concerned not with the reputation it brings, but how it helps its possessor 'by itself' (367d).

We have mentioned the likelihood that one of the charges on which the historical Socrates was tried was corrupting the youth of Athens. Following the contributions of Glaucon and Adeimantus, it is clear that Socrates' task in defending justice in the *Republic* is the opposite: to prevent the corruption of the youth of Athens by the cynical moral attitudes of their elders.

The City-soul Analogy (367e–369b)

Socrates claims to be in a quandary, lacking the ability to defend justice while nevertheless feeling compelled to do so (368b–c). His suggested solution begs a number of questions, though Adeimantus assents to it without demure. Socrates proposes that rather as someone with poor eyesight and unable to read small writing might be relieved to find a 'larger copy of the same writing . . . on some larger surface' (368d), so he will examine justice in the city as a whole and only then 'make a similar inquiry into the individual, trying to find the likeness of the larger version in the form the smaller takes' (369a).

The hypothesis itself is clear: it will be easier to determine the nature of justice viewed at the level of the city as a whole, since 'justice will be on a larger scale in what is larger, and easier to find out about' (368e–369a). Yet we are left to ponder the precise economy of the proposed analogy. Ought we to expect that whatever is true of the city as a whole must be equally true of all its individual human parts? Or need it only be true of the majority or a certain group? Indeed, is the analogy to be conceived in explicitly causal terms at all? Might we not understand it as a proportional relation, the city and the soul standing in a certain ratio to one another? We shall return to this matter in due course, as well as the charge that Socrates gives insufficient consideration to the grounds for the analogy, thereby creating insuperable difficulties in the argument as a whole.

The city-soul analogy also raises the question of the subject matter of the *Republic*. So far the discussion has concentrated on the identity of the just individual. The issue is whether the city-soul analogy re-establishes the discussion on a political rather than an ethical footing. One response is to suggest that the dichotomy itself is a false one. While we moderns may differentiate between an ethical and a political enquiry, the ancient Greeks did not. Hence, Adeimantus does not question the city-soul analogy because it reflects the conventional view that ethical questions are only properly addressed in a broader political context. Aristotle makes a similar point at the beginning of the *Nicomachean Ethics* (1094a–b).

However, one might reply that there is little in the dialogue to support this suggestion. If so, then we return to the original question: is the introduction of the analogy a pretext for shifting the focus onto political concerns? Or is the analogy merely a political means to what remains the ethical end of establishing the identity of the just individual? Though the latter is Socrates' stated purpose, the claim is often made that the *Republic* is principally a work of political philosophy, as we have already discussed. We shall consider the plentiful grounds for the political reading as we proceed. Though we have referred to it in the singular, it is to be emphasised that the political reading takes many different forms. Nonetheless, most share the premise that the account of the just city is proposed as a paradigm to which political reformers might aspire, and is to be assessed in these terms. (Unless specified, in what follows it is this approach, broadly conceived, to which the phrase 'political reading' refers.)

On the other hand, the reader should consider the possibility that Socrates is to be taken at his word. The most influential advocate of the ethical reading in recent years is Annas, who argues that the political reading obscures other important aspects of the dialogue. Annas focuses on the point that the expressed rationale for considering justice in the city is in order to illuminate the account of justice in the individual. Annas does not deny that the *Republic* contains political proposals; her aim is to challenge the view that the exposition of 'Plato's political philosophy' is the dialogue's centrepiece (see Annas 1999: 72–95).

The First and Second Cities (369b–376c)

We begin to see how these contrasting perspectives play out in the discussion of justice in the city. Socrates locates the origin of the city in the natural interdependence of human beings: 'we are not, any of us, self-sufficient: we have all sorts of needs' (369b). As a consequence, humans cooperate for the provision of these needs – food, housing, clothing and other necessities – each individual dedicated to the particular task for which they are naturally predisposed. Socrates' hypothesis contains a number of assumptions: (1) that nature predisposes individuals to perform a certain task (farmer, builder, tailor, and so on); (2) that nature allocates predispositions such that a community does not end up with a surplus of builders and a shortage of farmers; and (3) that each individual will carry out their naturally allotted task and no other. In short, Socrates' hypothesis assumes a natural division of labour – we shall refer to it as the 'principle of specialisation' – by which farmers, for example, produce food sufficient both for themselves and for those who, in the practice of their respective tasks, work to house and clothe not only themselves but also the farmers. Initially, Socrates appears to have a commune-type arrangement in mind, but it becomes evident that he envisages a basic market economy. There is trade both within the city and with other cities involving brokers and middlemen. Surplus production is exported in exchange for goods to fulfil the needs that cannot be met within the domestic economy.

His description completed, Socrates asks where 'justice and injustice' are to be found within such a city, and concurs with Adeimantus' suggestion that the most likely place is 'some sort of need which these people have of one another' (371e–372a). In short, justice seems to reside in the harmonious cooperation of the individuals that comprise the city, each fulfilling their specified role. But the point remains undeveloped at this stage. Instead, Socrates describes the way of life in such a community, a semi-rural idyll in which all basic needs are provided with only the most modest of additional refinements. It is the vision of a lost 'golden age' with which Plato's audience would have been very familiar: 'drinking wine after their meals, wearing garlands on their heads, and singing the praises of the gods, they will live quite happily with one another' (372b).

Glaucon brings this misty-eyed panegyric to an end, however, when he describes Socrates' community as 'a city of pigs', maintaining that 'if they are going to eat in comfort, they should lie on couches, eat off tables, and have the cooked dishes and desserts which people today have' (372d–e). Glaucon's intervention reflects the impatience of the urban sophisticate, appalled by the prospect of a life lacking the refinements to which he is accustomed. In their contrasting attitudes we see responses that are mirrored today in the contrasting reactions to radical environmentalist visions of a post-capitalist society, some of us enchanted by the prospect of a simpler life without the stresses and strains of the '24/7' society, others of us horrified by the prospect of a life stripped of its consumer comforts.

Socrates admits Glaucon's concern. 'We are not just looking at the origin of a city, apparently,' he remarks, but a 'luxurious city' with all the trappings of sophisticated urban living: 'incense, perfume, call girls, cakes – every variety of all these things' (372e–373a). An immediate consequence is the need for a dedicated army, since neighbours' territory will have to be expropriated and defended in order to secure the resources required to meet the luxurious city's swollen desires (373d–e). At 374e, the military are named as 'guardians', and it is agreed that they will have to be carefully chosen. Most importantly, to ensure that they are 'fearless and invincible in the face of any danger', they will need to possess a 'spirited' nature (375b). At the same time, they will need to be 'gentle in their dealings with their own people' (375c). Socrates suggests a questionable analogy with the disposition of the pure-bred dog and its ability to distinguish between friend and foe. Thus, in addition to spirit (*thumos*), the guardian requires a second quality: so as to know those to whom they should be gentle, they will need to be 'by temperament a lover of wisdom, a philosopher (*philosophos*)' (375e).

Concluding the sketch of the character of the guardians, Socrates turns to the provision for their education. Before following him, we shall consider the principal interpretative question raised by the separation of the two cities. Recall that while Socrates defers to Glaucon's demand on the grounds that it is in the second 'swollen' city that 'the point where justice and injustice come into existence in the cities' is most likely to be found, he maintains that the first city is the 'true city – the healthy version, as it were' (372e). This has prompted a number of commentators to ask why Socrates concedes Glaucon's point if it is in the 'true' city that we were poised to locate justice. I highlight this issue not least to illustrate how adopting a political or an ethical perspective on the dialogue can lead the reader along significantly different interpretative paths. For example, Nickolas Pappas explains the introduction of the second city on the argument that the perfection of the first city renders it 'the wrong entity to study from the point of view of developing a political philosophy'. Justice will only appear when it 'has the opportunity to contrast itself with the injustice possible in a more complex city'. Further, the second city is Plato's warning against reading the dialogue as mere 'fantasy'. In the transition from the first to the second city, Plato 'acknowledges and resists the temptation to utopia . . . Plato wants to produce a political philosophy not only rigorous in its theory, but also imaginable in practice' (Pappas 2005: 64).

Pappas' explanation makes sense if one has already decided that the city-soul analogy is the pretext for Plato to outline a political philosophy. Otherwise, it is less persuasive. White, for example, reads the purpose of the transition from first to second cities to be that of foregrounding the promised return to justice in the individual. When it is embodied, he suggests, the human soul possesses physical desires that crave the sort of luxuries introduced by Glaucon. Hence, 'the problem of controlling these appetites is parallel to the problem in a city of controlling citizens' appetitive cravings' (White refers forward to 435c–442d). On this reading, the rationale for the second city is not political; instead, its luxuries provide a 'parallel to the appetites in the individual'. Without the luxuries Plato would be 'unable to draw the analogy between the city and the individual that he needs' (White 1979: 88–9).

The Education of the Guardians (376c–412b)

Discussion of the guardians' education occupies the remainder of Book II and much of Book III. Socrates and Adeimantus – who now replaces Glaucon – agree that it is warranted since, as the guarantors of its security, the guardians are key to the city's survival. Still one might question the need for such an extended consideration. On the political reading, the fundamental role of education in the city's construction is evident only in retrospect, for it is more than an issue of guaranteeing the security of the state. As Socrates will emphasise at 423a–424b, the survival of the just city is wholly predicated on the maintenance of its education system. In this regard, it is important to observe that Socrates' city possesses none of the constitutional apparatus for limiting the power of its governors or for safeguarding the rights of its ordinary citizens that are demanded of a liberal democracy. In the absence of any such system of 'checks and balances', the education system bears the entire burden of ensuring the city is justly governed.

On the ethical reading, the extended nature of the discussion is explained in terms of the original pretext for the city-soul analogy, namely to illuminate the character of the just individual. Thus conceived, Socrates' proposals for education reveal much about the nature of that individual. At the same time, the discussion of education raises an important question: is it possible to conceive of the just individual outside of the just city? On the political reading, the answer is no: the conditions provided by the just city are necessary conditions for the growth of the just individual. The ethical reading, on the other hand, contends that the *Republic* is a defence of what is known as the 'sufficiency thesis': the argument that individual virtue is sufficient for happiness and that the conditions supplied by the just city are not a prerequisite for the existence of the just individual. For the strongest evidence to support this claim, we shall have to wait until the end of Book IX. By contrast, the assumption in Books II and III that education is central to the upbringing of the just individual would seem to present a significant obstacle to the sufficiency thesis, since one might ask where the education to produce the just individual could be found in the unjust city.

The education of the guardians is discussed in two parts: 'music and poetry (*mousike*) for the mind or soul' and 'physical education (*gymnastike*)' for the body (376e). Though this division of education follows convention, many of Socrates' subsequent proposals would have struck the original audience of the *Republic* as radical if not preposterous, a response that is echoed by many modern readers. Popper articulates a common response when he accuses Plato of advocating a system of censorship and rigid indoctrination reminiscent of totalitarian regimes (see Popper 1995: 53–5). Popper's charge cannot be dismissed, though one might counter that his determination to view the *Republic* as a template for Soviet Russia and Nazi Germany leads to interpretative extremes. In recent decades, scholars have sought to redress the balance by suggesting that, on some points at least, Socrates' assumptions are not so different from our own. The point is also made that the discussion must be viewed in its dialogical context, rather than as a fully articulated 'theory of education'. Having said that, it is difficult not to extrapolate from it, and Socrates himself often appears to speak as though his remarks are applicable to education generally.

Socrates first considers *mousike*, incorporating music and poetry but also other 'liberal arts': literature, history, philosophy, and so on. His focus is the literature that formed the backbone of a traditional education and to which the Greeks turned for moral and religious wisdom, most notably Homer and Hesiod. In this connection, it is important to bear in mind that Socrates' concern is moral rather than academic; for him it is a question of which literature will encourage the development not of intellect but of character, though at this stage the specific nature of the latter remains obscure. In short, the aim is to produce individuals who, when 'old enough for rational thought', will recognise the 'noble and good . . . because of its familiarity' (402a). A programme of what we may be minded to term indoctrination is required to fulfil this aim, since Socrates believes that children must only be exposed to what is 'noble and good'. In its turn this will require considerable censorship, given Socrates' belief that much of traditional Greek literature is wholly unsuited to the task at hand.

The first casualty is any story that misrepresents the gods (377e). Socrates argues that god – he moves freely between singular and plural deities – is good and so it is a deception to represent him doing anything unworthy. Hence, the many stories in which the gods fight among themselves or cause unwarranted harm must be cut (379a). The same fate awaits any story in which god changes his appearance or in any other way endeavours to deceive (380d–381e).

Further prohibitions cut huge swathes through the Greek literary canon, often with seemingly ludicrous effects (see, for example, 393e–394b). Only literature that exemplifies the desired qualities of character is permitted. The stories that survive minimise the fear of death (386b); exclude intemperate expressions of grief (387d) and of laughter (388e); encourage self-discipline (389d); and, but for those occasions when lying is a moral necessity, promote a respect for truth (389b). In addition, no story illustrating the thesis that injustice is more profitable than justice is allowed, though how literature represents the contrary thesis cannot be specified until the true nature of justice is determined (392c).

Having discussed the content of literature, Socrates considers its permissible forms. Here it is important to bear in mind that the recitation of Homer and Hesiod, often to musical accompaniment, constituted a key part of traditional Greek education; hence the discussion of music from 398c–490e largely mirrors the restrictions placed on literature. Socrates asks whether only narrative – indirect speech – or imitation (*mimesis*), or a combination of both, is to be allowed (392d). The principle of specialisation is invoked, and it is agreed that imitation in the manner of an actor is not part of the guardian's task for fear that if a child mimics immoral individuals, then 'enjoyment of the imitation' will give rise to 'enjoyment of reality', an eventuality both Socrates and Adeimantus claim to have witnessed (395c–d).

A child is only to act in imitation of 'appropriate models' (395c), and even then sparingly; narrative is the ideal (396e).

Following the consideration of music – 'rhythm and mode penetrate more deeply into the inner soul than anything else does' (401d) – Socrates turns to the provision for *gymnatike* (403c–412c). As the discussion of music complements the discussion of literature, so the discussion of physical education complements the discussion of *mousike* as a whole. To produce a state of physical conditioning on a parallel with the self-disciplined soul, emphasis is placed on 'simplicity' rather than 'variety and luxury' (404e). A tangential discussion follows about the requirement for doctors and lawyers (405a–410b). It is noteworthy for its opening assertion that the presence of a large number of law courts and clinics is usually a sign of a city in decline, for Socrates takes the opportunity to contrast this with the luxurious city that they have 'purged' in the course of the discussion of education (399e). The conclusion is that physical education is valuable not in itself, but in as much as it contributes to the healthy soul (410b). The aim is to ensure a balance within the individual of the traits required in a guardian: spirit and intellect (410d).

Are the charges of censorship and indoctrination well made? It is clear that much traditional Greek literature is heavily censored under Socrates' proposals. Indeed, on occasion one wonders whether Plato intends us to take the proposals altogether seriously (consider, for example, the bowdlerisation of Homer at 393e–394b). At the same time, one cannot ignore that Socrates is considering the education of the young, and while one may consider the extent of the censorship to be extreme, the fact of censorship itself is less contentious. Few in liberal democratic societies would advocate the removal of all restrictions on the access of children and young adults to certain types of visual and print material (pornography is a popular example). Yet what remains troubling from a liberal point of view is the degree to which the censorship envisaged by Socrates cannot simply apply to children. As Pappas observes, 'as long as anyone at all has heard the objectionable tales, eventually the children will hear them as well . . . In order to protect the young guardians, the entire city will have to change its use of poetry' (Pappas 2005: 70). Socrates will reiterate this requirement when he returns to the quarrel with literature in Book X.

As to the associated charge of indoctrination, it is not a question of the 'brainwashing' commonly depicted in science-fiction films about futuristic dystopias. Socrates does not conceive of individuals as blank slates on which anything might be inscribed if the conditioning is thorough enough. Rather, the discussion considers how to nurture naturally existing dispositions that might then be receptive to rational thought. To this end, children are not exposed to influences that might inhibit this development, Socrates insists. If one believes that *all* control over the influences to which a child is subject constitutes indoctrination, then Socrates is surely guilty as charged. But as with the issue of censorship, it is more likely the extent of the restrictions that we find unacceptable, since they leave little scope for the intellectual autonomy that liberal societies claim to value.

Socrates makes the interesting suggestion that exposure to influences not conducive to a child's development will result in desensitisation. As he says, the fear is that hearing about the horrific crimes committed by the gods will lead the young to believe that replicating them is nothing out of the ordinary (378b). Conversely, constant exposure to what is deemed 'noble and good' will ensure that nobility and goodness are viewed as the norm. Yet even if one sets aside concerns about the indoctrination involved, since the young are exposed to only one set of values, one might also question whether it is helpful for children to experience only what is noble and good. As Sayers puts it, 'in reality, the world is not always beautiful . . . and people are not always virtuous'. Consequently, the education of the guardians 'will be a poor preparation for the world as it actually is' (Sayers 1999: 40). For Socrates, on the other hand, exposure to vice and ugliness is not worth the risk, even when it is experienced at what might be considered the safe remove of literature. Unlike a doctor, who needs to have experience of being ill in order to be good at medicine, the guardian does not need to experience immorality. In order to understand the evil of injustice he will rely on 'theoretical knowledge, not on personal experience' (408d–409b).

A final point concerns Socrates' approach to the development of character: will it indeed prepare the individual's intellect for rational thought? Annas thinks not, questioning whether the guardian's intellectual autonomy will survive the exposure to such a rigid set of values. 'Why,' she asks, 'should people who are – crudely put – brought up to be moral conformists suddenly turn out to be intellectual path-break-ers in later life?' If children are to develop skills of critical analysis, then far from making them receptive to such skills, Socrates' proposals will only serve to stifle them. Such individuals, it is claimed, will only be fitted to the reception of further moral dogma (Annas 1981: 87).

Justice in the City and the Soul (412b–445e)

In its wake, it is worth recalling why the discussion of the guardians' education began. In the search for justice in the city, the luxurious city necessitated that a section of the population be charged with acquir-ing and defending the land required to provide for its luxuries. The education of this military class was then discussed. Socrates' subse-quent question is 'which of [the guardians] are to rule, and which [are] to be ruled?' (412b). In other words, the military class is subdi-vided. Allusion has already been made to a ruling group within the guardians at 389b–c, when Socrates refers to those who are permit-ted to lie for the benefit of the city as a whole, and again at 390a. Still it remains a key moment in the construction of the just city, and a potentially troubling one at that; the apparent proximity of the mili-tary to this new executive class might be thought to corroborate the suspicion of totalitarianism. Indeed, the ruling guardians are 'the best of [the guardians]'; those who are 'wise, powerful and above all devoted to the city' (412c). The origin of their devotion is a height-ened and unshakeable understanding that the city's interests are iden-tical to their own, and that they and the city stand or fall together. To ascertain whether they are among the best, guardians are to be sub-jected to a series of exacting tests (412d–414a). Again we observe the immense burden on the education system to guarantee the city's sta-bility, and ponder whether any system of education could possibly bear such a weight.

(a) The Just City (414b–434c)

The separation of a ruling class from the military is confirmed at 414b, when the latter are renamed 'auxiliaries' and redefined as 'defenders of the rulers' beliefs'. The just city now comprises three distinct groups or classes: (1) the farmers, businessmen and artisans who populated the first city; (2) a military class; and (3) those whose task is to rule. To assist the latter, Socrates makes an infamous proposal that has been a point of debate for centuries, with many readers horrified that Plato, the father of Western philosophy, should countenance such an idea. In a more self-confidently religious age, we may have shaken our heads and attributed it to Plato's paganism. Today, readers of a secular and liberal disposition are more likely to attribute it to Plato's illiberal politics (we shall discuss this matter in more detail in due course).

Socrates suggests that the city needs a founding myth, a 'single, grand [or noble (*gennaios*)] lie that will be believed by everybody' (414b–c). Rulers and auxiliaries will be told that their education was a dream, and that in truth they were formed 'deep within the earth' and released with the duty of protecting their city (414d–e). In addition, everyone will be told that god created them using a mixture of gold in the souls of those who are to rule, silver in the souls of the auxiliaries, and bronze and iron in the souls of the skilled workers (415a–c).

In a sense, the myth emphasises the meritocratic nature of the city. God demands that the closest attention is paid to the compound of metals in the souls of children. In the usual course of events, individuals will parent children of the same type as themselves. But it is imperative that when this does not occur, the child is relocated to the appropriate class: 'there is a prophecy, god tells them, that the end of the city will come when iron or bronze becomes its guardian' (415c).

The purpose of the 'myth of metals' is clearly to instil the belief that each individual's position in society is divinely ordained, and thereby part of the natural order. Conceived in terms of the need to guarantee unity in the city, its introduction is perhaps not as shocking as it first appears. Socrates recalls 382d, and the possibility that rulers will need to lie in the name of what is right, a passage which in turn alludes to Socrates' response to Cephalus (at 382c–d, Socrates asks Adeimantus: 'isn't [the 'verbal falsehood'] useful . . . to stop those who are supposed to be our friends, if as a result of ignorance or madness they are training to do something wrong?') Indeed, one might question whether the lie is indeed a lie at all: Socrates uses the form of a myth to convey what, on his account, is a fundamental truth about the natural division of labour and the cornerstone of the city's stability. At the same time, it might be argued that to hear the proposal for a lie, however 'noble', from the mouth of Socrates is on Plato's part little short of a betrayal of his mentor's legacy.

Socrates expresses doubts not because he is squeamish about prop-agating a myth, but from a concern about how it might be established (415c–d). He sets his doubts aside, however, and proceeds to outline how the rulers will live (415d–417b). To reinforce the habits formed through education, auxiliaries and rulers are not permitted 'any private property beyond what is absolutely essential' and will be com-munally housed and fed. To this end they will tax the rest of the pop-ulace 'an annual payment for their role as guardians which leaves them with neither a surplus nor a deficiency'. They have no need of material gold, since they have god-given gold in their hearts, and it is 'sacrilege' to mix the two together (416e). Anticipating St Paul, Socrates appears to view the love of money and the love of the divine as mutually exclusive. More specifically, Socrates' concern is the destructive effect that capitalistic rulers would have on the city's unity. Socrates also anticipates Karl Marx's belief that the accumulation of private wealth is the source of social division (and he thereby differs from the likes of John Locke, for whom property rights are natural and a source of security and social stability). Invoking the principle of specialisation once again, Socrates contends that 'once [the rulers] start acquiring their own land, houses, and money, they will have become householders and farmers instead of guardians'. They will view their fellow-citizens as potential threats, and when that happens both they and the city will be headed for destruction (417b).

Book IV opens with an objection to these arrangements. It speaks to Socrates' insistence at 412d that the source of the rulers' devotion is the identification of the city's interests with their own. Adeimantus observes that the rulers would appear to be excluded from any share in the city's happiness, whilst everyone else is flourishing: 'all they do is guard it', he observes (420a). Adeimantus raises an important ques-tion about the rulers' motivation to govern, to which Socrates will return in Book VII. For the moment, he sidesteps the matter of indi-vidual motivation, reiterating that 'our aim in founding the city is not to make one group outstandingly happy, but to make the whole city as happy as possible' (420b). Socrates argues that Adeimantus' con-ception of happiness as self-gratification is inimical to the happiness of the city as a whole: 'you mustn't start forcing us to give the guardians the kind of happiness which will turn them into anything other than guardians,' he insists (420e). If the city's farmers and potters were granted luxuries and told to work only when they felt so inclined, then they would cease to be farmers and potters. Likewise, if the rulers were granted luxuries, then they would cease to be rulers. The issue is not as pressing for most of the population, since they are only responsible for specific areas of activity in the city. But if the rulers were permitted to indulge themselves in this way, then it would be calamitous for the city, 'since they alone provide the opportunity for its correct management and prosperity' (420e–421b). This is not to suggest that the rulers sacrifice their personal happiness as such: 'if the city prospers and is well established,' Socrates asks, 'can't we then leave it to each group's own nature to give it a share of happiness?' 'I'm sure you're right,' Adeimantus concedes, and there the matter rests for the moment (421c).

With the city's unity in mind, Socrates turns to proposals for protecting it. He warns that the city must guard against excessive financial prosperity and poverty, since riches lead to indolence and poverty renders a skilled worker incapable of practising his craft, and both are causes of instability. Likewise, the size of the city must be limited, since exponential growth is also a threat to the unity of the whole (421d–423d). These additional requirements pale into insignificance, however, next to the reiterated need to maintain the education system (423e–424a). All 'radical innovation' must be avoided for fear of the city being 'destroyed accidentally' (424b). If the education system is eroded, then no amount of additional legislation will save the city from degradation (426e). A conservative attitude is also expressed in respect of religion: 'we don't know about this kind of thing,' Socrates counsels, 'and when we found our city . . . the only authority we shall follow, is the traditional authority', namely the pronouncements of Apollo emanating from Delphi (427c).

At 427d, Socrates declares the city founded, though it remains to identify justice and injustice within it. How this is accomplished leaves many readers dissatisfied. The first problem concerns the assumption that the city thus founded is 'wholly good', and as such 'wise, courageous, self-disciplined and just' (427e). In addition to the general question of whether Socrates' city is indeed the epitome of goodness, one might also ask the specific question of whether it self-evidently possesses these four excellences in particular and exclusively. In citing these four, Socrates appeals to the 'cardinal virtues' of Greek tradition, but in itself this establishes nothing. He further claims that identification of the first three excellences will, by a process of elimination, reveal where the fourth – justice – is to be found (427e). Yet we could only know that what remains is indeed the excellence we were looking for if all the possibilities have been surveyed, which they have not. Instead, it is tacitly assumed that no alternatives exist.

At least Socrates' *modus operandi* is clear. Wisdom (*sophia*) is the first excellence examined, and it is agreed to be the preserve of the rulers. Carpenters, sculptors, farmers and the like possess knowledge that is valuable to the city – namely, of their respective crafts – but it is not their knowledge that determines whether the city itself is wise. Echoing the point made at 421a–b, Socrates insists the knowledge possessed by the rulers 'makes decisions about the city as a whole' (428b–d). Similarly, the courage (*andreia*) possessed by the population viewed as a whole is irrelevant to locating courage in the city: 'no one classifying a city as cowardly or brave would look at any other part of it than the part of it which makes war in the city's defence, and serves in its army' (429b). Hence, the city's courage is the preserve of the auxiliaries, since in that part the city possesses 'a power capable of preserving it' (429c). The third excellence, self-discipline (*sophrosune*), differs from wisdom and courage in not being identified with a particular group. It is, Socrates suggests, 'a kind of order' (430e), specifically a type of self-mastery by which 'the better rules the worse' (431b). In the city it is reflected in the arrangement whereby 'the desires of the ordinary majority [are] controlled by the desires and wisdom of the discerning minority' (431c–d). Phrased otherwise, self-discipline is found in the agreement between rulers and ruled concerning who is to rule (431d–e). As such, it is relational: a 'harmony of some sort' that 'extends . . . throughout the city' (431e–432a). We note that there is no account of how this 'agreement' comes about – mention of democratic elections, for instance, are wholly absent – an issue that will resurface when Socrates considers whether the just city is a practical possibility.

Justice remains, though Socrates insists that 'it's been lying here under our noses all this time' (432d). It is located in the principle of specialisation that has guided the discussion of the just city from its inception (433a). Thus, the definition of justice is summarised as 'everyone performing his own task'. It relates to the other excellences,

Socrates contends, as 'the thing that gave all the others the power to come into being', and that subsequently sustains them (433b). Justice is the precondition of the other excellences: if the rulers rule, the auxiliaries protect, and the skilled workers practise their respective competences, then the city will be wise, courageous and self-disciplined. This conception of justice, Socrates insists, resonates both with a longstanding popular notion of justice (433a–b) and with legal justice, the latter also a matter of ensuring 'people's ownership and use of what belongs to them, and is their own' (434a). Lastly, its veracity is confirmed if the antithesis is examined. Socrates is not so much concerned with the shoemaker who attempts to do the job of a carpenter either in addition to or rather than his own, but with those who attempt to step out of their allotted class: the shoemaker who seeks to become a warrior, or the warrior who seeks to become a ruler (434a–b). If the latter were to occur, then it would destroy the city. In fact, no greater crime is imaginable – the reason it is labelled injustice and its opposite justice (434b–c).

(b) The Just Soul (434d–445e)

We shall consider the critical debates surrounding Socrates' account of justice in the city when the city-soul analogy is complete. Turning to the just soul, Socrates emphasises that the present account is provisional: 'if the same characteristic turns up in each individual human being, and is agreed to be justice there too, then we shall accept it . . . If not, we shall have to look for something else' (that is to say, return to the city and begin again) (434e–435a). Socrates proceeds on this methodological assumption, though a little further on he notes that an alternative method would surely yield better results. However, 'it is longer and more time-consuming' (435d). Socrates will recall this rather elliptical allusion later in the dialogue.

Hitherto Socrates has spoken of 'three types of nature' in the city, each performing a particular function (435b). Is the just soul similarly divided into three elements, each corresponding to a type of nature found in the city? At 435e, Socrates suggests that the soul must mirror the city, since the latter is nothing but the individual souls that comprise it, a further remark to which we shall have cause to return. The central question for Socrates is whether the activities characteristic of the different natures found in the city are practised in the individual soul with 'the same part of ourselves', or whether 'we do different things with different elements'; in short, whether the soul is simple or composite (436a).

Socrates pursues the latter hypothesis by distinguishing between rational (*logistikon*) and desiring or appetitive (*epithumetikon*) elements in the soul. To this end, he applies what, after Cross and Woosley, we shall term the 'principle of conflict', stated thus: 'nothing can do two opposite things, or be in two opposite states, in the same part of itself, at the same time, in relation to the same object' (436b) (Cross and Woosley 1964: 115). Accordingly, when something performs two opposite actions, the thing in question must contain multiple parts. Socrates anticipates Sigmund Freud's view that to understand the phenomenon of internal conflict is key to understanding human psychology. Socrates observes that when a man is standing still, but at the same time moving his head and hands, we do not properly describe him as 'at the same time both at rest and in motion.' Instead, we should say that 'one part of him is at rest, and another part of him is in motion' (436c–d). A complex argument follows in which the principle is applied to psychological conflict (437a–439e). The examples of hunger and thirst are offered, in which 'the soul of the person who desires something either reaches out for what it desires, or draws what it wants towards itself' (437c). There are cases, Socrates observes, when a thirsty person nonetheless desists from drinking. How are we to account for such phenomena? It follows not that the soul is performing the same movement in the same – single – element of itself, he replies, for that would violate the principle, but that the soul possesses separate elements: a desiring element pulling in one direction, and a rational element that for one reason or another – let us say that the individual suspects the drink to be adulterated – refuses to drink and pulls in the opposite direction.

To these two elements of the soul, a third – the spirited part – is added (439e). Following Glaucon's initial impression that the spirited element is akin to the desiring part of the soul, Socrates seeks to distinguish between the two with the story of Leontius. Following a public execution, Leontius desired to look at the corpses left beneath the city walls at the same time as he 'felt disgust and held himself back'. The desire to look won out, however – one might compare it to the conflict many people experience when passing a major road

accident – and he rushed over to the bodies saying to himself ' "there
you are, curse you. Have a really good look. Isn't it a lovely sight?" '
(439e–440a). The anecdote suggests that if the morbid wish to view
the executed bodies originates in the desiring part of the soul, then,
according to the principle of conflict, the competing impulse to resist
it – manifested in the angry feeling of disgust and moral indignation –
must originate in a separate element. The spirited part of the soul is
much more akin to the rational part, Socrates contends: rather than
'desirous in character . . . in the civil war of the soul [spirit] is far
more likely to take up arms on the side of the rational part' (440e).
This begs the question of whether spirit is indeed a distinct element,
or 'some form of the rational element' (440e). Glaucon advances his
own argument to establish its distinctness. Consider the case of young
children, he says, who are full of spirit from the time they are born,
yet who only later become rational. Socrates concurs, offering his own
example of animals – spirited but not rational – and a line from the
Odyssey: 'he smote his chest, and thus rebuked his heart' (*Odyssey*, Book
XX, line 17). Homer clearly portrays two elements in the soul,
Socrates insists: 'the part which has reflected rationally . . . has some
sharp words to say to the [spirited] element which is irrationally
angry' (441a–c).

Having distinguished the parts of the soul, Socrates declares that
they have 'made it to dry land' and agreed that the individual soul
'contains the same sorts of things, and the same number of them, as
a city contains': the rational part of the soul corresponding to the
ruling class; the spirited part to the auxiliary class; and the desiring
part to the artisan class (441c). What remains is to outline the excellences that enable the parts of the soul to fulfil their respective
functions, a task that occupies Socrates to the end of Book IV
(441c–445e).

He argues that, given the similarity between the structure of the
city and the soul, it follows that the excellences will similarly correspond. So, the individual will be 'wise in the same way, and using the
same part of himself, as the city when *it* is wise' and likewise for the
brave individual, both excellences belonging to a particular part of
the soul – the rational and spirited parts – just as in the city they are
proper to the ruling and the military classes respectively (441c).
Further, 'a just man is just . . . in the same way a city was just' when

each element of the soul performs its 'proper task' in accordance with the principle of specialisation. This involves the rational element ruling in the interests of the whole, Socrates specifies, with the spirited element as its immediate 'subordinate' and 'ally' (441d–e); the former making wise decisions that the latter uses its courage to put into effect (442b–c). In concord, these two elements 'will exercise control over the desiring element' that, in its craving to satisfy 'the body's so-called pleasures', would otherwise overwhelm the soul and destroy its natural unity (442a–b). Reflecting its role in the just city, the remaining excellence – self-discipline – is introduced as 'the result of the friendship and harmony' of the soul's three elements: 'the ruling element and the two elements which are ruled agree that what is rational should rule, and do not rebel against it' (442c–d).

To conclude this part of the discussion, Socrates returns to the excellence of justice, seeking to allay fears that it is incompatible with the 'everyday' conception of justice. It is inconceivable, he insists, that an individual, each part of whose soul performed its proper function, could be guilty of embezzlement, or indeed any crime or moral failing (442e–443b). No specific argument is offered to support this contention, but the implication is if an individual possesses a just soul, then the desire to steal, cheat, and lie will be controlled. Lest he be misunderstood, however, Socrates emphasises that justice is not characterised by just action. The principle of specialisation, according to which justice is the 'external performance of a man's function', was a useful 'image' of justice, but true justice is an internal condition of the soul, each element performing its own task 'like three fixed points on the musical scale – top, bottom and intermediate' (443c–e). Thus understood, a just action is one that, directed by wisdom, 'preserves or brings about this state of mind', while in its ignorance an unjust action destroys it (443e–444a). The unjust soul is then contrasted with the harmonious arrangement of the just soul. The former, Socrates says, is involved in a 'civil war' between the three parts of the soul, a 'rebellion of one part of the soul against the whole' that manifests the vices of injustice, indiscipline, cowardice and ignorance (444a–b). Just and unjust actions are akin to healthy actions in accord with nature and diseased actions that pervert the natural order, reflecting healthy and diseased souls respectively (444c–e).

Socrates marks the completion of the first part of the task set by Glaucon and Adeimantus by recalling what he has yet to do. Having defined justice and injustice in the city and the soul, he observes, it remains to determine 'which is more profitable' (444e–445a). The latter is straightforward enough, Glaucon suggests, since it is inconceivable that the possession of a diseased soul could be more profitable to its possessor than a healthy soul (445a–b). But Socrates insists that it is no time to rest on their laurels, and proposes to confirm the matter by examining 'what I believe to be the forms taken by vice (*kaka*)'. There are four such forms, he suggests, and at the beginning of Book IV he proposes to contrast them with the single form of excellence by discussing each as they manifest themselves in the city and the individual. He is about to proceed with this task when he is interrupted (445c–449b).

This is a sensible point to pause and consider some of the interpretative matters arising from Socrates' discussion of human psychology. One might first consider what Socrates means by 'soul'. The question first arises from the discussion of the function of the human soul at 353d, and Socrates will consider the immortality of the soul and describe it in recognisably religious – and markedly different – terms at the close of the dialogue. In the present context, it is reasonable to assume that Socrates speaks not of humankind's divine part, but of human 'personality' in general (though how this is to be reconciled with a religious account is uncertain). An additional problem is what is meant by 'parts' of the soul. In the present discussion at least, Socrates does not commit himself to the claim that the parts of the soul are topographically separate in the way that one might refer to different 'parts' of the body, though in the *Timaeus* that is precisely what happens (see *Timaeus*, 69b–72b). However, one might contend that it is equally unsatisfactory to assume with Cross and Woosley that the language of 'parts' is simply metaphorical since, like Freud, Socrates' argument for the division of the soul seeks to establish three actual and distinct sources of action (Cross and Woosley 1964: 128).

It is a complex question with implications for two further issues: the principle of conflict by which the parts of the soul are identified, and the specific nature of those parts. At first glance, the principle of conflict would seem to commit Socrates to a subdivision of the soul for each instance of conflict observed. However, a problem immediately arises in cases of conflict that one might otherwise attribute to the same part of the soul. Thus, to accommodate the case of the individual who experiences a conflict between the desire to eat and the desire to sleep would seem to necessitate a subdivision of the desiring part. Yet this is clearly not intended, since further divisions of the soul would destroy the analogy between the city and the soul. Socrates requires a neat tripartite division according to which the desires to eat and to sleep are placed together because they are self-interested cravings devoid of any consideration for what is prudent. By contrast, it would seem that the rational part of the soul is a purely cognitive source of practical judgement. The function of the rational part is to rule for the good of the 'entire soul' (441e).

Yet questions remain. While on the above account, the desiring part of the soul is conceived in terms of its selfish cravings, there is also the suggestion it is capable of exhibiting concern for the whole. Recall Socrates' statement that, in the self-disciplined soul, both the spirited and desiring parts 'agree that what is rational should rule, and do not rebel against it' (442d). It remains unclear how the desiring part of the soul arrives at a decision, implying cognitive activity of its own. Equally, while on the above account the rational part is characterised in terms of its cognitive function, there is also the suggestion that it possesses its own motivations. The rational part of the soul learns: it pursues knowledge (436a). It is also the part that seeks to discover whether we are suffering justly or unjustly (440c–d). Neither of these suggests that it is devoid of motivations of its own. The moot point is whether the argument that establishes the tripartite division of the soul can account for these ambiguities, or whether it collapses under their weight. If the rational part of the soul possesses its own motivations, then this complicates the characterisation of the desiring part of the soul as the part of the soul from which desires originate; it becomes the part of the soul in which only *certain* desires originate. Alternatively, if the rational part is purely calculative, and driven by passions that originate in the desiring part of the soul, then this would seem to compromise its status as the master of the desiring servant. Indeed, it would resemble David Hume's conception of reason as the 'slave of the passions' (Hume 1888: 415). As we shall see, these matters pertain not only to the question of the coherence of the account of the soul as it is presented in Book IV, but in the *Republic* as a whole: is the subsequent discussion of the soul consistent with the account offered in Book IV, or does Socrates radically revise the earlier account in the light of the turn that the dialogue is about to take? Nor, of course, are their repercussions limited to the definition of a specific concept; how we understand the soul has implications for how we understand the very nature of Socrates' just individual.

(c) Does Socrates Provide a Viable Account of Justice?

In the detail of the city-soul analogy, it is easy to lose sight of its original pretext: to meet the challenge of providing a viable account of justice. Does Socrates succeed? We shall consider three areas of contention: first, the relation between Socrates' conception of political justice and what we might term a liberal egalitarian conception of justice; second, the relation between the respective accounts of justice in the soul and in the city; and third, the relation between Socrates' account and the 'ordinary' conception of individual justice.

Faced with Socrates' formulation of justice in the city, readers often complain that it falls well short of the liberal egalitarian conception of justice. Fundamental to the latter is the principle that individuals are free to act as they wish in the fulfilment of their particular aspirations until doing so infringes on the freedom of others to do the same. By contrast, political justice in Socrates' just city is predicated on the principle of specialisation, which proscribes individual freedom of choice in the belief that the individual finds fulfilment in attending to his or her naturally allotted task. The charge laid at Socrates' door is that, in its denial of individual liberty, the 'just city' is the epitome of political *in*justice.

Since this objection is of a part with the charge of totalitarianism, we shall let it stand until we have considered the next part of the dialogue. Turning to the relation between the respective accounts of justice in the city and in the soul, there is a question mark over the compatibility of the two accounts. Note that this is less of an issue for the ethical than for the political reading. If, as on the ethical reading, the account of justice in the city is little more than a metaphor for justice in the individual, then the absence of precise parallels between the two accounts is not a major issue. But if, as on the political reading, the outline of the just city is as an earnest proposal for the ideal polity, then it is a different matter: a much closer correspondence between justice in the city and the soul is required.

As we have seen, the assumption behind the city-soul analogy is that the account of justice in the city will illuminate the account of justice in the individual only if the two accounts, in Bernard Williams' words, 'present the same message' (Williams 1997: 49). In a very influential essay, Williams contends that they do not. Williams' starting point is a particular interpretation of Socrates' claim that 'in each of us are found the same elements and characteristics as are found in the city'. Thus, the reason Athens has a reputation as a city with a love of learning is because its citizens possess a love of learning (435e–436a). Socrates is articulating the principle that a city is just if, and only if, its citizens are just, Williams maintains. The issue is whether this is compatible with the parallel claim that the soul is just when each part plays its allotted role, with reason dominating. In the city we find three classes of individuals in whose souls one part prevails over the other two, a different part dominating in the souls of the members of each class: reason in the rulers; spirit in the auxiliaries; and desire in the skilled workers. Yet it follows that only the rulers are in fact just in the just city, since only in the souls of the ruling class does reason prevail. The souls of both the auxiliaries and the skilled workers are unjust to the extent that they do not have the same ordering, which is precisely the reason why they are assigned to their respective classes. Contrary to the principle that a city is just if, and only if, its citizens are just, Williams concludes, only one class in the just city turns out to be just. Indeed, by far the majority of individuals in the just city are unjust, since the skilled workers comprise the greater portion of the population.

If one permits Williams' initial interpretation of Socrates' claim that 'in each of us are found the same elements and characteristics as are found in the city', then it is difficult to contest his conclusion. Ferrari argues that Williams misinterprets Socrates on the initial point. In attributing to Socrates the principle that a city is just if and only if its citizens are just, Ferrari contends, Williams falsely supposes that Socrates understands the city-soul analogy in terms of a causal relation. Yet given that Williams' supposition leads to the obvious problem he identifies – and given that the problem was as obvious to

Plato as it is to Williams – Ferrari suggests an alternative, namely that the city-soul analogy is understood precisely as an analogy. There is a parallelism between the city and the soul, and Plato intends it as such (Ferrari rejects the proposal that the political proposals are metaphorical). However, it is not causal but 'proportional': the just city and the just individual stand in a certain ratio to each other. In Ferrari's words, 'reason stands to the soul as rulers stand to the city, so that if reason is the ruler of the soul, then rulers are the reason – the wisdom or intelligence – of the city' (Ferrari 2005: 62). On this basis, he contends, Williams' criticism is not fatal to the city-soul analogy.

The issue concerning the relation between the Socratic and the 'ordinary' conceptions of justice is whether the former is at odds with the conception of justice held by Socrates' interlocutors. The debate usually takes its starting point from an essay by David Sachs, and articulates one of the main concerns of readers who are dissatisfied with the conclusion to Book IV. Socrates is guilty, Sachs argues, of the 'fallacy of irrelevance': Socrates agrees to establish the grounds for the ordinary conception of justice held by his interlocutors, but in the end he provides a definition of justice that bears little relation to it (Sachs 1997: 1).

It is important to clarify what is meant by the ordinary conception of justice. Sachs points to Thrasymachus' list of unjust acts at 344b – temple-robbery, kidnapping, burglary, and so on – the unjust acts of adultery, murder and usurpation that the shepherd carries out in Glaucon's story of the Ring of Gyges at 360b–c, and Socrates' own list of acts ordinarily conceived as unjust at 442e–443b (embezzlement, betrayal, neglect of parents, and the like). The point is that, as it is ordinarily conceived, justice consists in not committing such actions. Further, on the ordinary conception, justice is a matter of the relations between individuals and is a quality of certain actions. But, Sachs argues, Socrates' definition of justice shares neither of these aspects of the ordinary conception. As distinct from a quality of certain actions pertaining to the relations between individuals, Socratic justice is a state of mind – a 'relations of parts of the soul', as Sachs puts it – and as such beneficial to the individual in question (Sachs 1997: 14). Hence, the fallacy of irrelevance: Socrates' answer bears no relation to the question that provoked it.

Socrates, of course, is confident that he has established a relation between the two conceptions of justice, and cannot conceive how an individual with a just ordering of the soul could undertake any of the actions conventionally viewed as unjust. Yet, as we observed, no argument is provided to substantiate this claim; which is unsurprising, Sachs claims, for no argument would suffice. On Socrates' account, if the functions of the three parts of the soul are fulfilled, then the virtues of wisdom, bravery and self-discipline are exhibited, and the soul is just. But Sachs argues that wisdom, bravery, and self-discipline are 'compatible with a variety of vulgar injustices and evil-doing'. For example, one might show great wisdom, bravery and self-discipline in perpetrating a crime, and thereby on Socrates' account remain eminently just. Perhaps the best that can be said of Socrates' argument, Sachs concludes, is that 'crimes and evils could not be done by a Platonically just man in a foolish, unintelligent, cowardly or uncontrolled way' (Sachs 1997: 11).

Sachs' criticism has prompted a number of responses seeking to reconcile the Socratic with the ordinary conception of justice. I shall mention two of them, sketching them only in outline since it is not until later in the dialogue that they can be evaluated in full. The first, advanced by Richard Kraut, focuses on the idea that the just soul is committed to acquiring knowledge of what is for the good and acting in accordance with it (see Kraut 1992a: 311–37). Thus conceived, the just soul would not possess the sorts of desires that ordinarily lead to unjust actions because they are incompatible with the commitment to the good, and so the ordinary and Socratic conceptions of justice are reconciled. However, at this stage in the dialogue we are without an account of the good that would enable us to conceive of justice in this manner. On the account of justice provided in Book IV, the well-ordered soul could conceivably belong as much to the master criminal as to the paragon of moral virtue. Moreover, one might question whether it is necessarily the case that all unjust actions are motivated by desires that are incompatible with the rational desire for the good. What about the example of the individual who wishes to steal books in order to feed their desire for learning? It is not at all clear that, as it is conceived in Book II, it is incompatible for the just soul to possess both of these motivations.

The second response to Sachs – advanced by Annas – focuses on the idea that the just individual considers others in making moral decisions (see Annas 1981: 260–71). Socrates certainly has this in mind; at 412d, he makes the point – reiterated in response to Adeimantus at the beginning of Book IV – that the rulers are 'determined to do what is in the city's interests'. On this argument, the just individual is motivated to bring about what is good not simply for themselves but for the whole, and the individual acting in accordance with this motivation could never treat others unjustly by embezzling, lying, and so on, thereby reconciling the ordinary and Socratic conceptions of justice. Again, an account of the good is required before this response can be properly assessed, but this aside it already faces a potential problem. Socrates' task has been to show that it is in the interest of each individual to be just, and to this end he argues that the just soul is harmoniously ordered. Yet Annas' response to Sachs seeks to reconcile the Socratic and the ordinary conceptions of justice by arguing that the just individual has a commitment to the good of others as well as to their own. The question is whether our own particular needs and the good of the whole necessarily coincide. There are numerous conceivable cases, one might argue, in which one would have to sacrifice one's own good for that of the whole. To acknowledge them, however, would undermine Socrates' argument that it is in the interests of the individual to be just.

There seems to be a good deal more to say on the matter. In the event, Socrates does not disappoint.

Women and the Family (449a–471c)

Let us return to the beginning of Book V. In the relative wealth of its dramatic content, the beginning of Book V is reminiscent of Book I. Socrates is poised to examine injustice in the city and the soul when Polemarchus – silent since Book I – tugs Adeimantus' sleeve and whispers 'what shall we do? Shall we let it go?' (449b). 'It' refers to Socrates' remark at 423e–424a in the discussion of the rulers' lifestyle that 'friends will hold things in common', specifically women and children (449c). Adeimantus asks Socrates to explain himself more fully, supported by an apparently still grumpy Thrasymachus (see 450a–b).

Of all Socrates' stipulations for the just city, the matter of common ownership in general – recall that Polemarchus, for example, is heir to the family fortune – and of women and children in particular, would have seemed the most radical of all to Socrates' audience both inside and outside the dialogue. Viewed from an egalitarian perspective, ancient Greek culture was extraordinarily sexist, the wives, mothers, sisters, and daughters of Socrates' audience very much the private property of their respective husbands and fathers. As James Davidson observes, 'decent women in Athens were supposed to be secluded, avoiding the company of men outside the family and not even having their names mentioned in public' (Davidson 1997: 19).

Consequently, Socrates' reluctance to develop his proposals for public ownership comes as no surprise: 'I'd have been only too pleased if those remarks had been accepted as they stood,' he says, 'you've brought them up for examination, without the slightest idea what a verbal hornet's nest you are stirring up' (450a–b). Socrates will be proved right, not least in respect of the practicality of his proposals, a topic he broaches for the first time at 450c–d. Less clear are the grounds for complaining that, in requesting an explanation of the proposals for common ownership, his audience is 'taking us back to square one, to begin a second major discussion about the state' (450a). Adeimantus simply seems to be asking Socrates to explain a point of detail before proceeding with the discussion of injustice. However, Socrates' remark proves prescient.

(a) A Woman's Place: Is Socrates a Feminist? (451c–457b)
As though justifying it to himself, Socrates reflects that it was sensible to have considered the place of men before turning to that of women (451c). If we sense in this remark that women are reduced to an afterthought, then it must be set alongside the point that, given the cultural context, it is extraordinary that women are considered at all (at least on the proviso that Plato intends us to take the account seriously; see below). Aristotle, by comparison, has little to say about women in either the *Politics* or the *Nicomachean Ethics*, setting the tone for Western philosophy until well into the twentieth century.

The pressing question for Socrates is whether women should share the tasks of men in the public sphere, or remain in the home bearing and raising children (451d; restated at 453a). Glaucon's surprising response is that women 'should join in everything', though less surprisingly he immediately qualifies his remark by adding: 'we treat the females as weaker, though, and the males as stronger' (451d–e). Still it remains the case that women will share the education provided for men, notwithstanding the practical implications. For example, the Greek custom was for physical education to be undertaken in the nude, but if men and women are to be educated together, then the prospect arises of naked communal exercise. Socrates says that they should ignore the sniggering of those who are hidebound to social conventions, and instead listen to the dictates of reason (452c–e). Nonetheless, he proceeds to play devil's advocate to Glaucon's claim that women should share the tasks of men, invoking the principle of specialisation to suggest that women should undertake separate tasks from men because they have different natures. Reflecting the mores of the time, Glaucon does not seek to deny this even though it contradicts his original claim (453a–c). Indeed, Socrates adds, it was precisely to avoid such tangles that he was wary of broaching the issue of women in the first place (453d).

A way out of the dilemma, Socrates suggests, lies in specifying the '*kind* of natural difference or sameness' that applies in the case of men and women (454b). This is the crucial move in the argument. Socrates contends that biological difference – namely the fact that 'the female bears the children, while the male mounts the female' – is no more relevant to the question of whether a female might have a talent for medicine than being bald or hirsute is relevant to whether a male might prove a good shoemaker (454c–e). Although its egalitarian credentials are somewhat compromised by the appended suggestion that women are inherently weaker than men, Socrates' proposition remains as radical in much of the world today as it would have been in ancient Athens: 'none of the activities connected with running a city belongs to a woman because she is woman, nor to a man because he is a man. Natural attributes are evenly distributed between the two sexes, and a woman is naturally equipped to play her part in all activities just as a man is' (455d–e). Indeed, it is not only 'feasible' for women to rule if they are provided with the right education, it is 'for the best' (456c). A city possessing female leadership potential that is unrealised is a city that has departed from the principle of specialisation, and such a city is unjust. It almost goes without saying there is nothing better for a city 'than for it to have its women and its men alike become as good as possible' (456e).

A good deal has been written in recent decades on whether Plato's Socrates is a feminist *avant la lettre*. Much of the debate turns on what constitutes feminism. I shall distinguish between two feminist traditions, broadly conceived: (1) *egalitarian feminism*, characterised by a demand for legal, social and economic equality with men; and (2) the *feminism of difference*, characterised by an emphasis on the essential differences between men and women, and the need for women to develop a sense of female identity separate from the one granted by the dominant patriarchal culture.

The case for Socrates as a feminist of difference is relatively straightforward to assess. Recall that Socrates dismisses the relevance of biological difference, except to add that women are naturally 'weaker' than men, and so on average a woman cannot hope to fulfil a given role as well as a man. This is unlikely to endear Socrates to the feminist of difference, since his proposals seem to emasculate women as women altogether. With the erasure of biological specificity, Socrates denies women all the resources this might have provided for recovering a non-patriarchal sense of female identity. The equality granted to women in the just city only liberates women to the extent that they become diminished versions of men within what remains a patriarchal system, and for the feminist of difference this is no liberation at all. Women continue to incubate babies of course, but this biological role and the role that female rulers play in political life are wholly divorced from one another. In short, women become strangers to themselves.

The case for Socrates as an egalitarian feminist is more substantial. In the just city, Gregory Vlastos observes, female rulers achieve many of the reforms demanded by egalitarian feminists. Female rulers have equal access to education and to vocational opportunities; living communally with men, they have equal rights to unimpeded social interaction; they have the same legal and political status as men – men do not own women – and lastly they have equal access to sexual choice (neither men nor women have such freedom until they are beyond child-bearing age, after which the rules that govern their sexual relations are the same) (see Vlastos 1997: 115–28). The key point is Socrates' rejection of the traditional view that the woman's place is in the home, and that the public sphere is an exclusively masculine one. Aristotle criticises the proposals made in the *Republic* on precisely this point: if men and women are to follow the same pursuits, he asks, 'who will see to the house?' (*Politics*, 1264b). Aside from the insistence that, although nominally equal, women remain the 'weaker' sex, these are radical proposals given the status of women not only in ancient Athens but in Western culture as a whole until well into the twentieth century.

However, there is an opposing case to be made that also speaks from the perspective of egalitarian feminism. Annas, for example, argues that Socrates' proposals for women 'have nothing to do with women's freedom to choose their own way of life' (Annas 1981: 183–4). This is not because they deny women their identity as women – though they do – but because the motivation behind the proposals is fundamentally anti-egalitarian. Socrates' proposals are motivated not by an interest in the liberation of women, but because the city needs to utilise all of the talents at its disposal in order to be just. That the proposals only apply to a very limited number of women, namely those with the potential to become rulers, is symptomatic of this (here, as elsewhere, reference to those outside the ruling class is conspicuous by its absence). Annas makes the point that later in the dialogue Socrates will express his contempt for sexual equality when it is motivated by the democratic principle, a motivation that is shared by egalitarian feminism (see 563b).

It is a telling argument; further, it is interesting to observe that it applies not only to the position of women in the just city. To the extent that it highlights potential criticisms of Vlastos' case, Annas' argument pertains to the absence of male freedom as of female freedom, highlighting the restrictions on individual freedom for both sexes in the just city.

(b) Sex in the City (457b–461e)

Socrates and Adeimantus agree that they have survived the 'first wave' of criticism provoked by the proposals for female rulers, but await another provoked by the proposals for the common ownership of women and children (457b–c). All women 'shall be wives in common' for all men, Socrates declares. There will be no cohabitation, and 'children in turn shall belong to all of them', no parent knowing which children are their own and no child knowing the identity of its parents (457d).

Socrates acknowledges that these are the most radical proposals of all, though not so much for their desirability – he assumes that they would be of 'major benefit' to the city – as for their 'feasibility' (457d). Still he seeks to defer the question of their practicality in order to pursue the details of the proposals themselves (458a–b). Permission granted, Socrates describes the arrangements for policing sexual relations in the city (458c–461e).

Humans being humans, Socrates insists that communal living will inevitably 'lead them into having sex with one another' (458d). But this presents a problem that threatens to destroy the just city altogether. Sexual attraction cannot be allowed to determine who mates with whom, for erotic love (*eros*) does not have the interests of the city at heart. To ensure the 'quality of our herd', what is termed 'haphazard sexual intercourse' must be prohibited, to which end Socrates requires a further noble lie to ensure that only the best men have sex with the best women, and that other combinations are kept to an absolute minimum (458e–459e). 'Sacred' breeding festivals are proposed, at which suitable young men and women are brought together for the purpose of producing potential rulers. Partners are determined by a lottery system rigged to produce the desired couplings, the opportunity to sleep with more women a reward for men who excel in a particular area of endeavour. The resulting children will be removed from their mothers and transferred to a nursery in a separate part of the city, to be nursed by specialists (460c). Any child resulting from an unsanctioned union – along with any child suffering from a disability – will be disposed of in accordance with the traditional Greek practice of infanticide by exposure (460c). Further regulations concerning the reproductive prime of men and women are then made, before Glaucon raises the question of how, given the rules governing filial anonymity, incest is to be avoided, especially between fathers and daughters. Socrates suggests that all children resulting from a festival in which a given male takes part will refer to him as their father, while he in turn will call them his sons and daughters, though brother-sister unions will be permitted 'if that is how the lot falls out, and if the Pythian priestess gives her consent as well' (461d–e). It is clear that policing this system will represent quite a task for the guardians; someone will need to take a lot of notes.

For many readers of the *Republic*, the proposals for regulating sex in the city are abhorrent. Liberal societies in the twenty-first century generally conceive of marriage as a romantic expression of individual

choice based on profound feelings of erotic and emotional attachment. What is more, the horror of incest within our immediate family
is such that we rarely even speak of it. Socrates might contemplate the
prospect of incest between brothers and sisters with relative equanimity, but were we to rig the lottery it would be precisely to prevent
this eventuality. Bloom speaks for many when he writes that the effect
of the proposals is 'to remove whatever is natural in the family'
(Bloom 1991: 385). Readers are equally repulsed by the eugenicist
aspects of Socrates' proposals, reminiscent of Nazi plans for breeding a master race, and fictional dystopias such as Aldous Huxley's
Brave New World and George Orwell's *Nineteen Eighty Four*.

Those readers who do not find Socrates' proposals morally repug-
nant are more often than not too busy laughing about the levels of
observation required to enforce them, not least the prospect of a dedicated team of 'sex police' tasked with roaming the communal living
areas. Indeed, it is noteworthy that most commentaries spend little
time discussing this part of the dialogue. Cross and Woosley, for
example, devote less than two out of nearly 300 pages to 449a–471c
in its entirety (see Cross and Woosley 1964: 134–5). This might partly
reflect an indifference to feminism, but the lingering suspicion is that
they are simply embarrassed by the absurdity of Socrates' plans,
regardless of how integral they might be to the constitution of the just
city. It is also interesting to observe the advocates of the political
reading who choose not to dwell on Socrates' proposals for sex in the
city. Pappas, for example, devotes only a single page to them (Pappas
2005: 103–4). On reflection, one might incline to Waterfield's view
that much of the *Republic* 'is simply absurd if read as serious political
philosophy' – these passages being the most evident case in point –
and ask whether the reason this section of the dialogue receives such
little attention in certain commentaries is precisely to avoid detract-
ing from the view of the dialogue as a serious work of political philosophy (Waterfield 1993: xviii).

Having said that, there are other political readings that do give
equal weight to Socrates' proposals, seeking to head off criticisms such
as Waterfield's by questioning whether the proposals are indeed as
absurd as they might first appear. Sayers, for example, argues that the
ancient Greeks would not have been particularly shocked by Socrates'
proposals; arranged marriage was the norm, a means of ensuring

continuity in property inheritance and political alliances between families and tribes, and it remained so for centuries. (We romantic moderns are the historical odd ones out in this respect.) Further, Sayers argues that the idea of a planned society – long a taboo subject because of its association with Nazi eugenics – is no longer consigned to the realms of political fantasy. Developments in medical technology, he points out, 'are opening up eugenic possibilities far beyond anything ever dreamed of by Plato'. In Sayers' view, the *Republic* raises important questions that we ought not to ignore from moral squeamishness. Rather, in the spirit of Plato's rationalism, 'we should act in the light of the fullest available understanding of what is possible and what consequences will follow' (Sayers 1999: 89–91).

(c) The Problem with Families (461e–471c)

Having concluded the regulations governing sex in the city, Socrates considers whether they are consistent with other proposals for the just city. He recalls the definition of justice and injustice, reiterating that what is bad for the city is what divides it, while what is good for the city 'unites it and makes it one' (462b). Hence, the best city is one in which 'the greatest number of people use [the] phrase "mine" and "not mine" in the same way about the same thing'; or again, the city that most closely approximates an individual organism in which the experience of pleasure and pain in a particular part is experienced by the organism as a whole. Socrates offers the example of an individual who hurts a finger: we say that the individual rather than the finger is experiencing pain, for we understand the individual to constitute a single 'community' (462c–d). A city that possesses a similar degree of unity will likewise 'rejoice together or grieve together' (462e). This collective sense is achieved as a direct consequence of the provision for the common ownership of women and children, Socrates contends. Unlike other cities, in which members of the ruling class will be related to some of their peers but not to others – with all the potential for division that such a situation possesses – in the just city all of one's peers will be rightly called one's brothers and sisters, and one will behave accordingly (463e). Among other benefits mentioned, lawsuits and prosecutions between feuding individuals will 'virtually disappear' (464d–465e). The result is a happy city, contrary to Adeimantus' complaint at 419a that the rulers will be made distinctly unhappy by the way of life they are obliged to adopt (465e–466a).

An important implication of Socrates' conception of the just state as a single united family is the need to dissolve the traditional family unit. Interposing between the individual and the state, the traditional family provides an alternative focus for loyalty and sense of belonging – as most famously in the case of Antigone – and is wholly incompatible with the structure of the just state in which the individual identifies with the city as a single whole. The institution of the family further implies the separation of the public and private spheres, also incompatible with an arrangement requiring close public scrutiny of who is fraternising with whom. Aristotle first criticised this implication of Socrates' proposals, arguing that the abolition of the traditional family would erode rather than generate unity in the city. For Aristotle, the two qualities that inspire regard and affection are 'that a thing is your own and that it is precious'. But a society in which women and children are held in common is one in which everyone is equally one's own and equally precious. The result is that 'love will be diluted' – just as 'a little sweet wine mingled with a great deal of water is imperceptible in the mixture' – and a situation created that is contrary to the one intended (*Politics*, 1262a–b).

There is an interesting parallel between this and a debate in our own ethical and political discourse. In this regard, Socrates anticipates the liberal humanist who argues that our ability to identify with other human beings is capable of transcending the bounds of family, class, race and nationality; even that we have a moral duty to ensure that it does. Aristotle, on the other hand, is father to a strain of conservative thinking that views such arguments with suspicion, fearing that a naïve insistence on our duty to identify with humanity as a whole will have the practical effect of weakening our identification with those whom we can realistically hope to benefit.

Following the discussion of community cohesion in the just state, Socrates again raises the question of the feasibility of his proposals, only to embark on a consideration of how the guardians will prosecute war (466d–471c). It is 'obvious how they will go about it,' Socrates suggests (466e), though his proposals are without precedent. The most robust children will accompany the adults on campaign in order to observe the occupation that awaits them, acting as assistants in the meantime, but at a safe distance so that they can flee if neces-sary (466e–467e). Socrates adds various proposals regulating conduct in the field towards both friend and foe, making a strict distinction between the rules that pertain in conflicts with fellow Greek states – properly termed civil wars in which 'Greece is sick, and divided against itself' – and non-Greek 'barbarians'. In conflicts with fellow Greeks, there will be no enslavement of the vanquished, no wasting of each other's lands, and only those directly responsible for causing the dispute will be pursued (468a–471c). Glaucon agrees, but suspects that Socrates is avoiding the main issue and insists that he address how these proposals might be put into practice. We shall return to this point in the dialogue in a moment.

Is Socrates' Just City Totalitarian?

In the light of the proposals for women and the family, we can now return to the first area of contention regarding Socrates' conception of justice, namely that it is wholly at odds with a liberal egalitarian account; indeed, that Socrates' account of justice is the totalitarian epitome of political injustice.

The question is, of course, principally of interest to those who con-ceive the *Republic* as a work of political philosophy. If, on the other hand, one inclines to the ethical reading, and approaches the discus-sion of the just city as, in Waterfield's words, an 'extended metaphor' for the just individual, then the stakes are significantly lowered (Waterfield 1993: xviii). On the latter view, the totalitarianism debate misses the fundamental point of the city-soul analogy, repeated at 434d–e when Socrates reiterates that the discussion of the just city functions only in order to illustrate the account of the just individual. As Simon Blackburn observes, if the focus is on the just soul, then 'there is no room for a charge of totalitarianism, since it is surely harmless to urge that it is the well-being of the whole totality, the whole agent considered in all his or her mental aspects, that is the aim' (Blackburn 2006: 81). (The point is well made, even if certain 'post-modern' conceptions of the self might contest its basic premise.) However, the problem with the ethical reading – especially in Waterfield's radical formulation – is that it is obliged to find metaphorical significance in each and every proposal for the just city, and this is a tall order. Perhaps it is the case that, in Blackburn's words,

'Plato *relishes* the details of his state, and gives far more than he can transport back into the analogy with the mind' (Blackburn 2006: 57). If so, then the political reading returns to the fore, and with it the issue of the totalitarian character of the just city.

The standard bearer for the claim that the *Republic* is a textbook for totalitarianism is Popper. His argument focuses on two aspects of the just city: first, the strict division of classes, in particular the separation of the ruling class from the rest; and, second, the identification of the city's fate with that of the ruling class and the subservience of all other interests to ensure the city's unity is maintained. From these defining characteristics, Popper derives others: the monopoly on military values and education possessed by the ruling class; the extensive censorship and propaganda exercised by that class; and the city's self-sufficiency, isolating it from external influences. At every turn, Popper contends, the just city flatly contradicts what he terms the 'humanitarian theory of justice': to the principle of egalitarianism it opposes the principle of natural privilege; to the principle of individualism it opposes the principle of collectivism; and to the principle that the state's purpose is to preserve the freedom of its citizens it opposes the principle that the citizen's purpose is to preserve the unity of the state (Popper 1995: 100). In short, 'Plato's political programme . . . is fundamentally identical with [totalitarianism]' (Popper 1995: 93).

Popper makes a powerful case, but it is by no means the final word. I shall focus in particular on the issue of freedom. Much of the rhetorical force of Popper's case derives from the central claim that, whilst in the 'open society' the individual is free, in the just city freedom is sacrificed to the need to maintain the unity of the city as a collective. But is the matter quite so simple?

Again, much depends on how terms are defined, in this case 'freedom'. Popper's argument assumes the liberal definition of individual freedom as the ability to determine one's own interest, and to pursue it without hindrance to the point that one infringes on the freedom of others to do the same. A city is just in as much as it protects this freedom. Accordingly, the collectivism attributed to Socrates' city proscribes freedom in so far as it imposes a shared interest – the unity of the city – that is pursued to the exclusion of the individual interests of its citizens. In as much as this is accomplished, Socrates' city is unjust. Yet one might argue that Plato's Socrates would not recognise the disjunction in Popper's argument between individual and collective interests. While there is some debate about whether or not the rulers sacrifice their own happiness in the just city, Socrates clearly does not advocate the systematic sacrifice of individual interest in the name of a greater unity. On the contrary, Socrates envisages a political arrangement whereby the interests of each individual are scrupulously observed in accordance with the principle of specialisation. The unity of the just city, the argument runs, does not require the sacrifice of individual interests; it depends on their realisation. The difference between Popper's 'open society' and Socrates' just city is not the difference between a society that protects freedom and one that proscribes it, one might conclude, but the difference between alternative conceptions of freedom.

This is an important point, though as such it does not absolve Socrates of the accusation of totalitarianism. To the extent that it does not allow the individual to determine what is in his or her own interests, instead investing all such power in a ruling class, the just city remains steadfastly totalitarian. However, rather than the extreme totalitarianism that Popper ascribes to the *Republic*, C. C. W. Taylor argues that the lesser charge of paternalism is more accurate. On Popper's account, Socrates' city is totalitarian because the interests of the individual are subordinated to the interests of the collective. Taylor suggests that the just city is more fairly described as paternalist since, conceived in these terms, 'the priority is reversed. The function of the state is simply to promote the welfare of its citizens, the welfare being defined independently in terms of such individual goods as knowledge, health and happiness' (Taylor 1997: 34). While it remains broadly authoritarian, it is specifically paternalist since the happiness of the city is not something over and above the happiness of the individual; rather, the happiness of the former is comprised of the happiness of the latter. The perfectly organised city is subordinate to the happy community.

A similar effort to extricate the just city from Popper's analysis is made by Sayers. Maintaining that the just city does not so much crush individuality as offer 'an account of individuality as essentially social', Sayers contends that the dialogue offers a 'form of communitarianism' (Sayers 1999: 53). It is an excessively authoritarian form of communitarianism that views all expressions of autonomy as a threat to social unity, he concedes, but it is one in which a positive model might be found, and it remains relevant today as an antidote to liberal individualism.

As is clear, in neither of Taylor nor Sayers' responses to Popper is it a question of wholly rejecting the thesis that Socrates' city is authoritarian. Instead, the aim is to resist the tendency to equate what is outlined in the *Republic* with the twentieth-century experience of Nazi Germany and Soviet Russia. Both would certainly concur that the *Republic* is not a defence of any form of liberal democracy. But is the latter possibility to be dismissed out of hand? An interesting alternative is available to those readers who agree with Waterfield that the *Republic* has little to offer as a work of political philosophy, but who at the same time find the ethical reading – especially in Waterfield's extreme formulation – ultimately unconvincing. The thesis is most closely associated with the twentieth-century American philosopher Leo Strauss, though it has been pursued by a number of others, most prominently Allan Bloom. In essence, it agrees that the *Republic* is a dialogue in which an authoritarian system of government is outlined, but contends that Plato's purpose in doing so is ironic: the aim is to highlight the preposterousness of the just city. On this view, the proposals for women and the family are a case in point: 'Book V is preposterous,' Bloom writes, 'and Socrates expects it to be ridiculed' (Bloom 1991: 380). In fact, Socrates defends a broadly democratic position. (Thus, strictly speaking, it is also a political reading, though one that views the proposals for the just city as dystopian rather than utopian.) We shall have cause to return to this highly controversial reading when we consider Socrates' account of the democratic city and soul in due course.

Books V–VII (471c–541b)

We shall now turn to the remainder of Book V (471c–480a) and Books VI–VII, concluding at 541b. For many, this portion of the *Republic* – less the discussion between 521c and 541b – constitutes the heart of the dialogue. So much so, it is often studied on its own. Defenders of this strategy observe that 471c–541b comprise an extended digression, beginning with Glaucon's insistence that Socrates examine the practicality of his proposals for the just city, and concluding with Socrates' return to the task set aside at 449c of describing injustice in the city and the soul. Consequently, it can be wrested from the whole without leaving too many thematic loose ends. The way is further eased if one assumes that the dialogue form is a vehicle for Plato to expound a particular philosophical thesis, with Socrates as his mouthpiece. For if so, then qualms about compromising the dramatic unity of the dialogue may be set aside in the pursuit of 'Plato's philosophy'. In this respect, it is especially significant that 471c–541b contains Socrates' discussion of the so-called 'theory of the forms', since a popular rationale for isolating this part of the dialogue is in order to concentrate on what is generally viewed as the cornerstone of Plato's thought. In the hands of the best scholars, it is an approach with much to commend it, yielding rigorous and illuminating accounts of the epistemological issues raised in the *Republic*.

And yet, it remains the case that isolating 471c–541b risks obscuring more than it illuminates. While this portion ostensibly comprises a digression, to follow the numerous strands of Socrates' discussion demands detailed acquaintance with what precedes it. Ultimately, the middle books of the *Republic* are best read as part of the whole to which Plato evidently intended them to belong.

The 'Third Wave': Is the Just City Possible? (471c–474b)

Having heard Socrates' proposals for the conduct of war, Glaucon's patience runs out. He demands to know 'whether it is possible – and just *how* it is possible' for the just city to become a reality (471c). Socrates declares his reluctance to face a 'third wave' of criticism – 'the largest and most threatening of the three' – following those that greeted first his remarks on women, and then on the status of the family (472a). But Glaucon stands firm, insisting that he 'stop playing for time, and tell us' (472b).

Socrates only relents when Glaucon acknowledges that putting theory into practice was not part of the original agreement. Rather, 'we were looking for . . . a model [*paradeigma*]' (472c). Socrates draws an analogy with the artist who 'paints a picture which is a model of the outstandingly beautiful man . . . but is unable to show that it is possible for such a man to exist' (472d). Glaucon concedes that the inability to establish how the just city might be brought about does not detract from the validity of the model or ideal itself, before

Socrates adds a final point: it is 'natural', he says, that practice is less perfect than theory (473a). Glaucon allows that it is a matter of the degree to which the just city is approximated (472e–473b).

The exchange is noteworthy on a number of counts. On the political reading, we are now deeply immersed in the detail of Plato's political philosophy. In particular, the concession extracted from Glaucon has a bearing on the charge – made most forcefully by Popper – that Socrates' account of the just city is a piece of naïve and politically dangerous utopianism. On Socrates' account, the just city is a theoretical 'model' to aspire to on the understanding that, in practice, it can only ever be imperfectly realised. The point does not wholly absolve Socrates of the accusation of naïve utopianism – as distinct from the lesser charge, so to speak, of idealism – but it might blunt some of the more simplistic claims that are made in this connection. On the ethical reading, attention might be drawn to Socrates' comments at 472c–d, in which he explicitly refers the debate over practicalities back to the question of the 'perfectly just and unjust man'. One might argue that, if not for Glaucon then for Socrates at least, the principal issue remains not the city but the individual.

His point accepted by Glaucon, Socrates braces himself for the 'largest wave' that is sure to follow the suggestion that only a 'single change' in contemporary society is required for the just city to be realised. If it is a solitary change, however, it is a singularly momentous one:

There is no end to suffering, Glaucon, for our cities, and none, I suspect, for the human race, unless either philosophers become kings in our cities, or the people who are now called kings and rulers become real, true philosophers . . . It is hard for people to see that this is the only possible route to happiness, whether in private life or public life. (473c–e)

As Socrates predicted, Glaucon is taken aback by this suggestion. He presumes to speak for the audience as a whole in replying that Socrates' proposal is little short of an incitement to violence. 'Can you hold them off,' he asks, 'find an argument to escape by?' (474a).

We might wonder why Glaucon is so astounded by Socrates' proposal. Does it reflect the contempt in which Athenian society held the philosopher? Or has it to do with the radical nature of the proposal itself, and an assumption that philosophy and politics are incompatible? The prospect of Socrates suffering violence, and the contrast between the threat of physical force and the power of speech, might be an allusion to the exchange between Socrates and Polemarchus at the beginning of the dialogue. Alternatively, it might be an allusion to the ultimate fate of the historical Socrates at the hands of the restored democrats. Such possibilities aside, the introduction of the philosopher clearly leaves Socrates with much to explain, not least on the political reading. For example, it raises the question of the compatibility between the proposed 'philosopher-ruler' and the preceding account of justice in the city. As we have seen, the just city is founded on the principle of specialisation: 'one man, one job'. But Socrates' insistence that the just city can only come about if rulers become philosophers and vice-versa, predicates the realisation of the city on the seeming injustice of a single individual with, in effect, two jobs (philosophy and political rule). On this account, Socrates faces a considerable task. For the just city to possess a just philosopher-ruler, Socrates has to show not that philosophy and political rule are compatible roles – that the philosopher ought to rule because he is best qualified to 'multi-task' in this way – but that they constitute one and the same role. It might be argued that, if this cannot be substantiated, then on Socrates' own account the possibility of realising the just city is severely compromised (see Pappas 2003: 116–17; Sheppard 2004: 35–6).

Thus conceived, it is an especially worrisome problem on the political reading. On the ethical reading, by contrast, one can afford to be far more sanguine about any breakdown in the city-soul analogy that the introduction of the philosopher might be said to herald. Hence, Annas contends that, while it is not explicitly stated in the dialogue itself, the introduction of the philosopher is Plato's way of drawing a line under the analogy and any pretence of an integrated account of justice in city and individual. The account of the just city 'remains . . . effective as an ideal to stimulate virtue in individuals', rather than 'as a blueprint for any real society'. While 'justice in the state is an all-or-nothing affair, individual justice is a matter of degree'. On this view, the need for Socrates to show that the account of the philosopher-ruler is wholly compatible with the definition of justice in the city falls away. The just city can be left to stand as an ideal, 'whereas [Plato] wants individuals actually to improve by reading the *Republic* and using it as an ideal to which to conform themselves'. In the figure of the philosopher-ruler, the centre of attention remains the individual (Annas 1981: 187). Yet this raises its own issue, companion to the issue faced by the political reading. For while the question of the philosopher-ruler's compatibility with the definition of justice in the city may fall away, there remains the question of the philosopher-ruler's compatibility with the definition of justice in the individual. I shall characterise it in terms of a distinction made by Terence Irwin: is the just individual to be conceived on the 'practical' model of the philosopher we find in Book IV, the guardian for whom reason is primarily concerned with harmonising the different parts of the soul into a unified whole? Or is the just individual to be conceived on the 'contemplative' model of the philosopher to which we are about to be exposed, the lover of wisdom for whom reason is primarily concerned with obtaining knowledge of abstract metaphysical truths? (See Irwin 1977: 234–7.)

Who is the Philosopher? (474b–487a)

Socrates begins by defining the philosopher. He focuses on the etymology of *philosophos*, a compound of *philia*, meaning love or friendship, and *sophia*, meaning wisdom. Hence, the philosopher is literally the 'lover of wisdom'. All lovers, Socrates asserts, love the object of their desire in all its aspects and manifestations. In other words, they love the 'whole class of things' rather than simply 'one particular example of it' (475b). It is a debatable point, to say the least. Socrates himself draws the parallel with the lover of wine who, he insists, loves 'any wine, for any reason' (475a). Yet this is manifestly not the case: the lover of wine loves good wine and dislikes bad wine. Still, Glaucon concedes the analogy, and only raises an objection to Socrates' conclusion that, as a 'lover of all wisdom' – rather than 'of one kind of wisdom, but not of another' (475b) – the philosopher, like the insatiable and undiscriminating lover of food, is 'ready to taste all learning' (475c).

Before examining Glaucon's objection, it is worth observing Socrates' focus on the philosopher as one who *desires* wisdom, since it raises the fundamental question of whether the account of the soul implicit in the discussion of the philosopher-ruler is compatible with the explicit account of the soul in Book IV?

For many readers, the answer is yes: it is clear in Book IV that the rational part of the soul possesses its own desires, namely the desire for knowledge. In corroboration, one might cite the passage at 375e, where Socrates describes the guardian as 'by temperament a lover of wisdom'. On this interpretation, there is no significant disjunction between the account of the guardian's soul in Book IV and the account of the philosopher's soul in Book V: Socrates always conceives of the guardian of the just city as a philosopher (see Annas 1981: 109–52).

However, it is a different matter altogether if, on one's reading of Book IV, the rational part of the soul does not possess any desires of its own, but is purely calculative. On this view, the introduction of the philosopher in Book V as the 'lover of wisdom' represents a discontinuity in Socrates' account of the soul and, by extension, the accounts of the guardian and the philosopher-ruler. But if this is so, then how is the inconsistency to be explained? Perhaps Plato wishes the digression between 471c–541b to complement the preceding discussion as part of a single argument, but fails on this point (Pappas 2003: 117–8). On the other hand, perhaps the 'digression' is not a digression within a single argument at all, but marks a new stage in an evolving discussion. In John Sallis' version of this 'dialectical' approach, the contention is, as the argument stands at conclusion of Book IV, Socrates the philosopher realises he has constructed a just city in which the 'lover of wisdom' has no place (Sallis 1996: 378).

(a) The Philosopher and the Forms (475c–476d)

Let us return to Glaucon's objection to the characterisation of the philosopher as a 'lover of all wisdom . . . ready to taste all learning' (475c). On this basis, Glaucon observes, all manner of individuals might be considered philosophers, not least 'all those who love to be spectators . . . They behave as if they had rented out their ears to listen to every chorus they can find. So they do their round of the festivals of Dionysus, never missing one, either in town or country'. Dashing from place to place, intent on gaining a glimpse of every festival in progress, such people wish to be acquainted with everything that is going on, and yet 'they wouldn't willingly go anywhere near a philosophical discussion' (476d).

Glaucon's 'spectators' – an alternative translation is 'lover of sights and sounds' – represent a cultural stereotype that traverses the centuries: the exhibition-goer who spends no more than a minute in front of any one painting, or the tourist who 'sees Europe' by spending no more than a day in each of a handful of capitals and a French vineyard. Thus conceived, the spectator represents a superficial minority from whom the rest of us quickly distance ourselves. Yet, in due course, it will become apparent that it is the philosopher, not the spectator, who is the exception. Indeed, the class of spectators will come to include anyone who does not fit Socrates' very particular definition of the philosopher. Contrary to Glaucon's characterisation, it will include a great number of readers who consider themselves most willing to engage in philosophical discussion.

Socrates' response takes account of my initial objection to the definition of the wine lover, since he differentiates between 'real philosophers' and those who merely resemble them; rather as one might distinguish between the discriminating wine connoisseur and the wine consumer who will drink more or less anything. Significant for what it reveals about the identity of the philosopher, the argument also introduces us to the 'theory of the forms'.

Socrates begins by securing Glaucon's agreement that the 'form' or 'idea' of beauty has a counterpart in the form of ugliness; likewise the just and the unjust, the good and the bad. Though a pair, Socrates adds, each form is itself 'one'. However, it is not as themselves that forms appear to the senses. Instead, forms 'appear all over the place, through their association with various activities and bodies and with one another, each [giving] the appearance of being many' (476a). In other words, what the spectator sees and hears is not the form of beauty as such, but the appearance of beauty in the plurality of beautiful paintings, melodies, actions, and so on.

The true philosopher is identified in terms of the distinction between the form in itself and the form as it appears to our senses. Whilst spectators take pleasure 'in beautiful sounds and colours and shapes, and in everything that is created from these elements', nevertheless 'their minds are incapable of seeing, and taking pleasure in, the form of beauty itself'. In short, spectators experience beauty through the senses as 'many', but do not experience beauty through the intellect as 'one' (476b). The true philosophers, on the other hand – Socrates emphasises that they are few in number – are 'capable of approaching beauty by itself, seeing it just by itself'

(476b–c). Socrates is not suggesting that the philosopher sees the form of beauty as an additional object of sensory experience, as though the philosopher might enter a gallery and see the form of beauty next to a beautiful painting, while the spectator sees the beautiful painting alone. Nor is the contrast between the spectator who experiences beauty solely through the senses – though this is indeed the case – and the philosopher who bypasses the senses altogether, and experiences the form of beauty solely through the intellect. The point is clarified in what follows. The spectator lives in a dream, incapable of under-standing whether an object resembles another object or whether it is that object: incapable, that is, of distinguishing between an image and the original from which the image is taken (476c). By contrast, the philosopher is awake and thereby able to make this distinction. In Socrates' example, the philosopher is able to 'look both at [beauty itself] and at the things which share (*metechein*) in it [namely, different beautiful objects] without mistaking them for it or it for them' (476d). In sum, the true philosopher does not see beauty through the intellect and, as such, to the exclusion of the senses. Both the philosopher and the spectator experience the same visual sensation. The difference is that the philosopher alone understands the single form of beauty in which those perceptions 'share' or – in an alternative translation of *metechein* – 'participate'.

So, the philosopher understands forms whilst the spectator – by implication the rest of us – does not. But what are forms? And why is knowledge of them key to the philosopher's competence to rule? Note that forms are introduced without a formal argument for their exis-tence (though such arguments might be constructed from later stages in the discussion, as we shall see). Further, Socrates does not adopt a single term to refer to them. On occasion, he speaks of the form as an *eidos*, but he also uses the synonym *idea*. Alternatively, he speaks of '[beauty] itself', or simply '[beauty]' in the singular, implying the 'one' form of beauty as distinct from the 'many' beautiful objects. We recall the point that Plato does not have an established philosophical vocabulary on which to draw; rather, we are witnessing the birth of philosophy itself. It also raises the question of whether it is accurate to speak of a 'theory of the forms' at all. Ultimately, it is we, and not Socrates or Plato, who refer to the discussion of the forms in the *Republic* as though it constituted a theory of knowledge. Having said that, perhaps the forms are introduced without a formal argument on the assumption Plato's audience is already acquainted with a theory he has explained in other dialogues or in the course of his teaching at the Academy. Or again, perhaps the explanation is Plato views the existence of forms as self-evident. It is a difficult matter to resolve. Whilst it is not illegitimate to construct a theory of knowledge from Socrates' remarks about the forms – to which end the discussion in the *Republic* constitutes one of the richest resources in all Plato's works – it is necessary to bear in mind that it is not as such a theory that the forms are discussed.

Concerning the nature of forms, there are a number of points on which we can so far be relatively confident: (1) forms are singular ('one'): the form of beauty is the only form of beauty; (2) forms are exemplary: the form of beauty is the perfect instance of beauty; and (3) forms do not appear to the senses as forms: what appear to the senses are the multifarious objects and activities that, as the philosopher alone understands, 'share' in the forms. As themselves, forms appear to the intellect alone. Still, many questions remain. We know little for certain about the scope of the forms. Hitherto, Socrates has referred only to justice, goodness and, his favourite example, beauty. Is the scope of the forms restricted to abstract concepts of this kind, or are there forms of physical objects (for example, is there a form of the vase in addition to the form of beauty in which the beautiful vase participates)? If forms are limited to abstract concepts, are there only forms of the 'positive' terms that have so far been mentioned – beauty, justice, good – or are there forms of their respective 'negative' terms: ugliness, injustice, evil? At 476a, Socrates implies that there are, but we may have reason to revisit this judgement. Finally, we know little of the precise relation between the forms as they are and the forms as they appear to the senses. At 476c, Socrates implies that the beautiful object 'resembles' the form of beauty as the image resembles the original, and at 476d that the former 'shares' or 'participates' in the latter, but it is unclear what these terms signify. However, we shall soon be in a position to answer an important question concerning the ontological status of forms (are they intellectual constructs, or do they exist independently of the mind that conceives them?). In addition, Socrates will endeavour to explain why knowledge of the forms qualifies the philosopher for political rule.

(b) Knowledge, Belief and Ignorance (476d–480a)

Having described the philosopher as awake while the spectator dreams, Socrates determines that the philosopher's state of mind, 'because he knows, is knowledge' – *gnosis*, but at 477b, *episteme* – 'while that of the spectator, because he merely believes, is opinion or belief (*doxa*)' (47bd). Socrates anticipates a disgruntled response from his notional spectator, affronted by this characterisation, and so proposes an argument that will establish the point to everyone's satisfaction (476d–e).

There follows a complex discussion in which Socrates links cognitive states to ontological categories. The opening premise is that the philosopher, as one whose cognitive state is knowledge, knows 'something that is', while the cognitive state of ignorance (*amathia*) is of 'something that is not' (476e–477a). The second premise proposes an intermediate ontological category 'whose nature is both to be and not to be' (477a). This in turn requires a corresponding cognitive state, namely belief. 'So belief is directed at one object, and knowledge at another, each according to its own particular capacity (*dunamis*)' (477b).

Before proceeding, Socrates clarifies the latter term. A capacity, he says, is 'what make[s] us capable of doing whatever we are capable of doing'. For example, sight is a capacity because it enables us to see (477c). Thus, capacities differ according to their respective objects and effects: 'any capacity which is directed at the same object and has the same effect, I call the same capacity, and any capacity which is directed at a different object and has a different effect, I call a different capacity' (477c–d).

The principle is then applied to the distinction between knowledge and belief. Each cognitive state is a distinct capacity, Socrates contends, belief as 'the thing that makes us capable of forming beliefs', and knowledge, by implication, that which makes us capable of knowing (477e). It follows that each is directed at a different object. Clearly, knowledge is 'directed at what is, and consists in knowing things as they are' (478a). As to the object of belief, it cannot be directed at 'what is not', since that is the object – or the non-object, for it is nothing – of ignorance. Nor does its object lie 'beyond the limits' of knowledge and ignorance, exceeding the former in its clarity or the latter in its obscurity (478b–c). It must lie at an intermediate point, sharing 'in being something, and in not being something' (478e).

On this basis, Socrates formulates a question for the hypothetical spectator 'who thinks there is no beauty in itself' (479a). Socrates asks whether the spectator would deny that the numerous objects that appear to the senses to be beautiful could on occasion appear to be ugly; similarly, that what appears to be just could also appear to be unjust, what is holy appear unholy, what is big appear small, what is light appear heavy, and so on. (Socrates' suggestion is that how a given appearance in a given context is characterised depends on that context: what is deemed beautiful in one context might be deemed ugly in another.) No, Glaucon replies, the spectator would have to concede that, in each example, 'they must necessarily appear to be both' the one and its opposite (479a–b). In which case, Socrates continues, there is nowhere else to locate these appearances than at the 'mid-point between being something and not being something', less obscure than what is not, while lacking the clarity of what is. It is probably in this intermediate zone that most people's standards of beauty and the like will be found 'rattling around' (479c–d). In accordance with Socrates' original distinction, such individuals will have to be content with the designation 'lovers of opinion,' since they 'take pleasure in and enjoy the things belief is directed at', namely objects of sense experience that can as soon appear beautiful as ugly. Only those who 'take pleasure in and enjoy the things knowledge is directed at' – namely 'the things themselves . . . always the same and unchanging' – deserve the title 'lovers of wisdom or philosophers' (479e–480a). Their standards of beauty, as of goodness and justice, do not 'rattle around', changing with the context in which objects appear. The philosopher sees things not as they appear but as they truly are.

In the interpretation of this passage, a great deal turns on how we understand the phrases 'what is' and 'what is not'. The question arises because Socrates uses one word – *einai* – where we ordinarily speak of 'is' in at least three different ways that are relevant to the present context: (1) the existential use of 'is' as in '*x* exists': the book 'is' in the sense that the book exists; (2) the veridical use of 'is' as in '*x* is true': the law of gravity 'is' in the sense that it is true; and (3) the predicative use of 'is' that ascribes a property to *x* as in 'the cup is white'.

Importantly, it is not a matter of obliging Socrates' use of 'is' to fit neatly into one or another of these uses, for he draws on all three at different points in the discussion. Instead, it is a question of which enables us to obtain the clearest understanding of the argument as a whole.

Cross and Woosley contend Socrates uses 'is' in its existential sense. In saying that knowledge is of 'something that is', Socrates means that knowledge is of 'the real or existent' in contrast with ignorance, 'whose object would be the utterly non-existent'. Knowledge is knowledge of forms as objects that exist (Cross and Woosley 1964: 45). But there are significant problems with this reading, as Annas observes in a very influential discussion of this issue. Most importantly, it would appear to commit Socrates to the notion of degrees of existence: 'what is' as that which wholly exists; 'what is not' as that which is wholly non-existent; and that 'whose nature is both to be and not to be' as that which exists to a degree. The problem is how to conceive of degrees of existence. It is certainly not a question of denying that forms are real; as we have seen, Socrates uses the notion of 'resemblance' to describe the relation between forms and their many manifestations, which certainly seems to suggest that the former are indeed 'more real' than the latter (see 476c). Nonetheless, whatever is meant by the talk of degrees of being, Annas contends, 'it cannot be degrees of existence'. Existence is a binary concept: an object either exists or it does not (Annas 1981: 196).

Initially, the veridical sense of 'is' seems more promising, since knowledge clearly is of 'what is' in the sense of 'what is true'. The problem here is how to conceive of belief. To assume that a given belief is either true or false is to run up against the problem of how to understand the object of belief as both 'what is and what is not'. Alternatively, to assume that the object of belief is intermediate between 'what is' and 'what is not' is again to confront the problem of understanding degrees, now degrees of truth. While certain modern epistemological theories may entertain such a notion, it is difficult to find corroboration for it in the *Republic*.

Annas turns to the predicative sense, and there finds the most suitable alternative: 'what is' should be read as 'what is F' where 'F' is a predicate or property such as beauty, justice or goodness. This makes sense of the claim that only 'what is' can be known, since something can only be known to possess the property of beauty if indeed it 'is beautiful'. Further, it makes sense of the claim that only 'what is' without qualification can be known without qualification, since only what is beautiful without qualification – 'always the same and unchanging' – can be known without qualification to be beautiful. Socrates appears to underline this reading a little further on, when he confirms Glaucon's observation at 477e that, unlike belief, knowledge is 'infallible'. To know something to be beautiful is to be certain of it. By contrast, belief is fallible because its object, which both 'is' and 'is not', is not always the same and unchanging. While in one context an object may appear to possess the property of beauty, in another it may equally appear to possess the property of ugliness. To believe something to be beautiful is to be uncertain of it, since the judgement is always subject to revision: the object considered beautiful in one culture or during a certain epoch may be considered ugly in another culture or during a different epoch, and so on. In short, no object of belief possesses a given property without qualification.

Crucially, the predicative reading avoids the problem of comprehending degrees of existence or of truth in relation to objects of belief. Having said that, it leaves us with the problem of how conflicting properties such as beauty and ugliness can be co-present in the same object (see 479d–e). Socrates' own examples are well chosen in this regard. We understand how a given country might be said to possess the properties both of largeness and smallness in the sense of being large in relation to one of its neighbours, and small in relation to another. The same applies to the properties of beauty and justice, for while they are not relational in the same way as largeness and smallness, we might argue that their possession is contextual, as suggested above in relation to the example of what is considered beautiful in one culture but ugly in another. Yet other types of property would seem to create a considerable problem for Socrates' argument. Annas offers the example of the property 'man'. On Socrates' argument, each particular man is also a not-man. As Annas observes, however, 'nothing can be, even qualifiedly, both a man and a not man' (Annas 1981: 209). One explanation of why Socrates' argument cannot accommodate such properties is that this was not Plato's intention. There is no form of man – and other such properties – because the scope of forms is limited to oppositional terms such as beauty, justice, goodness, and so on. But this possibility begs its own questions. If one can only know the forms, but there is no form of man, then one cannot know that a particular man – Socrates, for example – is a man. Such a conclusion would seem to leave us with a highly circumscribed conception of what can be known. Further, on the political reading, it begs the question of how knowledge of the forms qualifies the philosopher for the task of political administration if it is strictly limited to knowledge of abstract oppositional concepts.

We shall attend to Socrates' discussion of the philosopher-ruler's qualifications to rule in a moment. Before we do, it is important to observe that the foregoing discussion has decisively answered the question of the ontological status of the forms. Rather than intellectual constructs, forms possess a reality independent of the mind that conceives them. The moot point is the nature of that existence: what is the 'being' of forms? On the traditional dualist interpretation assumed by many commentaries on the *Republic*, 'what is' and 'what is not' inhabit wholly distinct realms of being: an original, necessary and immutable metaphysical realm of forms accessed only through human intellect, and a degraded, contingent and mutable physical realm accessed through the senses, the latter 'participating' in the former. Only the philosopher possesses knowledge of the realm of forms: ordinary human understanding is confined to the physical or empirical realm of mere belief.

The dualist or 'two worlds' interpretation is an enduring one for which much textual evidence might be adduced, as we shall see when we consider the analogies of the sun, the divided line and the cave. However, according to its advocates, there is an alternative interpretation that rescues the *Republic* from what Friedrich Nietzsche identified as the 'nihilistic' implications of the dualist reading. For Nietzsche, Plato's dualism is nihilistic because the opposition of a separate realm of immutable forms to the realm of mere sensory experience denudes the latter of any inherent meaning and value. The mutable realm of appearances is merely a debased version of a realm of forms in which true value and meaning reside ('we *revenge* ourselves on life by means of the phantasmogoria of "another", a "better" life,' Nietzsche writes). As Nietzsche conceives it, the task for philosophy is a 'revaluation of values' that dismisses the realm of forms as a chimera, and seeks to return value and meaning to the realm of appearances (see Nietzsche 1990: 39). And yet if, on Nietzsche's conception of this revaluation, Platonic thought is precisely what philosophy has to 'overcome', there is a strain in post-Nietzschean philosophy that instead views Plato's thought as a potential resource in this task. This is possible if the dualist reading of Plato – which Nietzsche sees as definitive of Western metaphysics as such – is not the only possibility available.

The most influential formulation of the non-dualist reading of Plato has its origins in the work of the twentieth-century German philosopher Martin Heidegger (see Heidegger 1991: I, 162–87). According to it, the language of distinct 'realms' of being is metaphorical. Socrates' discourse on the forms implies the existence of a *single* realm that reveals or shows itself in *two* ways. In the words of John Sallis,

on the one hand, a showing in which an *eidos* shows itself as it itself is, as one, as the same as itself; on the other hand, a showing in which it shows itself as many, in which it shows itself as it is not, in which it shows itself as being different from itself.

The distinction between these two 'modes of showing', Sallis maintains, 'is more fundamental than the distinction between the "intelligible" and the visible' (Sallis 1996: 385). Hence, the difference between the philosopher and the spectator is not that the philosopher is able to access a separate ontological realm, rather that the philosopher penetrates the surface of a single realm of being and understands things as they really are.

(c) The Attributes of the Philosopher (484a–487a)

At the beginning of Book VI, Socrates declares the account of the philosopher complete while acknowledging there are other matters to address 'before we can see how the just life differs from the unjust life' (484a). Attention turns to the philosopher's suitability to rule, in particular the relevance of possessing knowledge of timeless and unchanging forms to the administration of a temporal, mutable entity such as a city. The problem is particularly acute on the dualist interpretation since, if knowledge is limited to a separate realm of forms, then the particulars of political life can only be objects of belief. The philosopher-ruler can know what the form of justice is, but he can only possess opinions about whether this or that policy is just. Why is it necessarily the case, then, that the philosopher is more capable of ruling than the spectator?

Socrates begins his answer by securing Glaucon's agreement that the best guard is the one with the best eyesight. As the philosopher and the spectator were once characterised in terms of one who is awake and one who dreams, a parallel is now drawn between the sighted and the blind: as the blind cannot see, so those 'lacking in knowledge of everything that is . . . have no clear pattern or model in their soul' (484b–c). The philosopher, by contrast, who knows the forms and thereby possesses such a model, is compared to the artist who is able to refer to the model being painted. In formulating 'rules about beauty, justice and goodness in everyday life' – or defending those that exist – the philosopher is able to refer to knowledge of the forms of beauty, justice and goodness (484c–d). Hence, philosophers should rule, for while they cannot know that a given policy or rule is just, on the basis of their knowledge of the form of justice, they can determine which rule most closely resembles or most extensively participates in the form of justice.

Yet the philosopher's qualification to rule does not alone reside in the ability to make this sort of theoretical judgement. The philosopher is also 'the equal of the others in experience of practical affairs, and not inferior in any other area of human excellence' (484d). The task is to explain how such individuals come to exist (485a). On those political readings concerned with the compatibility of the philosopher-ruler with Socrates' account of justice in the city, this is a significant assignment, since the incorporation of the philosopher into the just city would seem to hang on its success. Recall that it is not simply a matter of explaining the advent of the individual who possesses knowledge of forms, and who in addition also happens to possess the excellences required to be a good ruler. If the principle of specialisation is not to be breached, then Socrates must show that philosophy and ruling constitute one and the same role. In other words, Socrates must establish that knowledge of the forms implies possession of the additional attributes in and of itself.

To this end, Socrates reiterates that the philosopher 'is always in love with any learning which helps to reveal that reality which actually is' – namely, forms – and loves the whole of that reality rather than particular parts (485a–b). Such a love implies 'a hatred of false-hood, and a love of truth' (485c), he contends. The nature that truly loves learning without loving truthfulness is inconceivable; it must possess the virtue of honesty (485c–d). In addition, the love of learn-ing implies an enjoyment of intellectual pleasure that steers its pos-sessor away from the pursuit of physical pleasure. As Socrates puts it, 'in someone whose stream [of desire] flows in the direction of learning . . . the desires will be concerned with the pleasures of the mind alone. They will give up the pleasures arising out of the body' (485d). This in turn will make philosophers self-disciplined and without avarice, since individuals are motivated to make money in order to provide themselves with lavish sensual pleasures (485e). A further implication of the concern for 'the wholeness and totality of things – divine and human' is that philosophers will lack meanness of spirit and small-mindedness (486a). Rather than focusing on an indi-vidual aspect of reality, giving it undue prominence in relation to the whole, they will always view matters in perspective, always view the 'big picture', so to speak, and this will extend to concern for their own lives: 'even death won't seem frightening to someone like this,' Socrates asserts (486a–b). Hence, the nature of the philosopher will also make such an individual courageous, and Socrates concludes that, taken together, it is impossible that 'this well-ordered person – who is not avaricious, not mean-spirited, not a charlatan or a coward – could turn out to be a contract-breaker, or unjust' (486b).

Besides moral attributes, the ideal philosopher also possesses certain intellectual skills, which Socrates enumerates in turn. The love of learning will make the philosopher quick to learn (486c): it is incon-ceivable that one who loves all of reality could possess a bad memory, since there is so much to remember, and a bad memory would be dispiriting (486c–d). Finally, a love of truth will lead to a sense of refinement and proportion (486d).

It is important to observe that Socrates considers the natural rather than the developed disposition of the philosophical individual in this enumeration (see 485c and 486a). As he points out at 487a, it remains to be established that the individual who possesses not only a natural philosophical disposition but who is also appropriately educated will be the individual best qualified to rule. Socrates is about to proceed with such a proof when he is interrupted.

The Status of the Philosopher in Contemporary Society (487b–502c)

It is now Adeimantus' turn to expresses frustration. Socrates' method of argument, he concedes, is very persuasive. By stages, Socrates convinces his interlocutors of the worth of his argument and the worthlessness of their own. 'They are like beginners playing draughts against experts,' he observes. And yet, it 'does nothing to convince them that the truth is as you say' (487c). The present discussion is offered as a case in point. While Socrates' account of the human excellences inherent in the philosophical nature is convincing as a theory, experience suggests that 'the majority of those who go in for philosophy . . . turn out to be extremely odd, not to say thoroughly bad'. For even the best of them, Adeimantus concludes, the effect of studying philosophy 'is to make them useless to their cities' (487c–d). How can such figures be the saviours of the city?

This is a direct challenge to Socrates' claim that the philosopher is the best qualified to rule. Adeimantus' scepticism explains Glaucon's astonishment at 473c–e: philosophers are not much use for anything, and ruling least of all. On the political reading, Adeimantus' interjection also restates the challenge made to Socrates at the beginning of the digression: to bridge the gap between theory and practice in relation to the just city. Even if Socrates satisfactorily accommodates the ideal philosopher-ruler in the ideal city, the question remains of how the ideal is to be approximated in practice.

(a) The Analogy of the Ship (487d–489d)

It is necessary to be clear what Socrates seeks to achieve in his reply to Adeimantus, for he does not dispute the claim that most of those who currently 'go in' for philosophy turn out to be useless to the city (487e). Instead, he responds to the charge by accounting for Adeimantus' perception of philosophers. In other words, Socrates provides a sociological account of why society holds the philosopher in such contempt. To this end, an analogy is deployed to which it is important to pay attention on two counts: first of all, the immediate context of Adeimantus' challenge; and secondly, the broader context of a political topic we have yet to broach: Socrates' assessment of democracy.

Adeimantus is asked to imagine the city as a ship, and its citizens as the ship's owner or captain, 'larger and stronger than everyone in the ship, but somewhat deaf and rather short-sighted, with a knowledge of sailing to match his eyesight' (488a–b). The political class are represented by the ship's crew, 'quarrelling among themselves over captaincy of the ship, each one thinking that he ought to be captain, though he has never learnt that skill' (488b). It is a democratic scenario in which the citizen electorate is theoretically sovereign, but in practice is unfit to exercise authority, and relies on politicians to advise it. In differentiating between the electorate and politicians, the analogy might be thought more reminiscent of a representative system of democracy than of Athens' system of direct democracy, by which each citizen was entitled to speak in the Assembly. However, we know there existed in Athenian society a group of public speakers who made speeches on behalf of the different sides in a debate. It is they who represent the crew in the analogy.

Socrates emphasises the lack of consensus among the crew as to what advice should be given to the captain. The root of the problem is quickly identified: none of the squabbling crew possesses the true skill of captaincy required to guide the ship, indeed no one believes such a skill can be taught (488b–c). The ship's crew are evidently a political variation on the theme of the spectator who does not believe in the forms and who is captivated by sensory experience, since the different factions among the crew press their claims not in the name of truth, but of power. As Socrates proceeds to reveal, their motivation for seeking power is to 'immobilise the worthy captain with drugs or drink or by some other means, and take control of the ship, helping themselves to what it is carrying' (488c). In short, their motivation for entering politics is the opportunity it affords for self-aggrandisement and the satisfaction of material desires.

The result is a radically unstable situation forever teetering on the brink of civil war: 'sometimes, if others can persuade him and they can't, they kill those others or throw them overboard' (488c). In such a system, the figure esteemed by the crew is the arch manipulator: 'good at finding them ways of persuading or compelling the ship owner to let them take control' (488d). The 'real ship's captain', on the other hand, who 'must of necessity be thoroughly familiar with the seasons of the year, the stars in the sky, the winds, and everything to do with his art' (488d–e) – and who evidently represents the philosopher in possession of knowledge of the forms – is ignored.

Significantly, the true captain does not only appear useless to the likes of Adeimantus; he is useless, since on the democratic ship of state the natural order is inverted: 'it is unnatural for the captain to beg the sailors to come under his command,' Socrates maintains: 'it is not up to the ruler, if he really is any good, to beg those he is ruling to *be* ruled' (489b–c). By right they ought to be asking him, as the only one who possesses the knowledge to captain the ship. But in this situation, the true captain does not find his natural and rightful place. He is surplus to requirements, condemned by his peers as a 'useless stargazer' (489c).

In this way, Socrates accounts for Adeimantus' perception of philosophy students. However, in view of the account of democracy that will be offered in Book VIII, it is worth considering the nascent critique of democracy contained in the analogy.

There is much in the analogy of the ship that might be applied to the twenty-first-century experience of democracy: an ill-informed electorate every bit as deaf and short-sighted as Socrates' own, and dissembling politicians whose aim is not truth but office and the material benefits that accrue from it. One might also recognise the factional and adversarial nature of political debate in the quarrelsome crew, and see the 'spin doctor' and special advisor in the archmanipulator. Against this, it might be argued that in drawing such parallels one is allowing oneself to be seduced by Socrates' cynicism. One might counter that, in twenty-first-century liberal democracies, the electorate as a whole is better educated and has access to more information than at any time in history, and on a regular basis acts independently of the advice of its political masters. The political scramble for power witnessed during election campaigns may seem undignified, but to suggest the lust for power is politicians' sole motivation, and politicians only seek to serve their own personal interests is unjustified. On the whole, politicians believe in the truth of what they say and endeavour to pursue the common good. Further, it is inaccurate to describe Western liberal democracies as forever poised on the brink of civil war and tyranny. It does not do to be complacent about such matters, but the 'separation of powers' in constitutional democracies – executive, legislative and judicial – is precisely designed to prevent democracy collapsing into tyranny. Least recognisable, perhaps, is Socrates' suggestion that democracy is a perversion of the natural order. As a rule, we hold with equal certainty the contrary view that democratic liberty is a natural right. In Isaiah Berlin's words, 'to be free to choose, and not to be chosen for, is an inalienable ingredient in what makes human beings human' (Berlin 1969: 122).

(b) The Analogy of the 'Large, Powerful Animal' (489d–502c)

If the occasion for the analogy of the ship is the uselessness of philosophers, then the analogy of the 'large, powerful animal' – sometimes referred to as the 'analogy of the beast' – addresses the second part of Adeimantus' challenge: 'why it's inevitable that most of those who go in for philosophy will turn out to be villains' (489d). It is a specific challenge to Socrates' conception of the philosopher as a paragon of human excellence.

In reply, Socrates points out that those who possess the requisite attributes are, perversely, most susceptible to corruption. As with any living thing, he asserts, 'if it cannot find the nourishment, climate and habitat appropriate to it, then the stronger it is, the more completely it fails to develop its potential' (491d). The philosophical nature possesses the potential for great evil as much as for great goodness, and if it is corrupted by the wrong education, then it will turn out very badly indeed (491e). Conversely, if it receives the requisite course of study, then 'I assume it can't help growing and coming to all manner of excellence' (492a). As to the wrong education, it is not individual sophists who corrupt young men, but the general public who, acting like a collective sophist, deluge the young philosopher in a 'torrent of disapproval and approval' until he adopts their views. Given the punishments the public can impose on any who refuse to bend to their will, Socrates asks, how could anyone possibly be expected to resist? The only possibility of the philosophical nature emerging unscathed is through 'divine dispensation' (492a–493a).

Socrates' complaint is a familiar one: popular opinion has a corrosive effect on the standard of public debate. In the words of Oscar Wilde, 'public opinion exists only where there are no ideas' (Wilde 1999: 1242). In a democracy, the result is that the politician's skill lies in catering to the wishes of the lowest common denominator. Hence, the sophist offers to teach 'exactly the same opinions as those expressed by the general public in its gatherings' (493a). The analogy follows in illustration: 'it's rather like someone keeping a large, powerful animal, getting to know its moods and wants'; over time, the individual would learn how to handle the animal, how to pander to its various desires. Eventually, the individual could systematise that learning and then 'take up teaching' (493a–b). Yet such a skill would be oblivious to which of the desires of the animal 'was beautiful or ugly, good or bad, just or unjust'; ignorant of its true nature, the good would simply be equated with what best pleased the animal (493b–c). The purveyor of this skill is much like the democratic politician who believes that 'wisdom consists in having identified the diverse moods and pleasures of the general public in its gatherings'. For the politician 'it's a question of "needs must when the devil drives". He has no option but to do whatever the public approves of' (493c–d). Consequently, the corruption of the philosophical nature is all but inevitable (494a).

Viewed as accounts of democracy, there is an interesting contrast between the two analogies. In the ship analogy, the electorate are depicted as the dupes of manipulative politicians. In the animal analogy, on the other hand, the electorate are depicted as a collective desiring machine to whose cravings the politician must respond if he is to retain his position. This aside, the latter analogy reiterates the points made in its predecessor: in a democracy, reason is usurped by desire, and the true nature of the good is sacrificed to the satisfaction of material wants. Again, there is much we might claim to recognise: politicians formulating policies on the basis of focus group research rather than a coherent political agenda and pandering to the whims of a certain section of the electorate instead of leading public opinion. Having said that, it might be argued we only tend to level this accusation when the government does not follow the policy our personal focus group would have them adopt. Nonetheless, we hold as a fundamental principle that the ruled should choose their rulers; to recall the earlier reference to Isaiah Berlin, it is essential to our sense of what it means to be human. Ultimately, it might be said, we approve of the vision of democracy offered in the animal analogy. We are comfortable with the idea that the skill of the democratic politician lies in following the wishes of the electorate, for we reject both the possibility of a natural elite in possession of a skill of absolute ends, and Socrates' contention that the wishes of the electorate are not in some measure informed by reason.

Of course, it is precisely the latter assumption Socrates contests. Where Socrates would seem to be less certain is whether democratic electorates get the politicians they deserve: the ship analogy suggests they are victims, the animal analogy suggests otherwise. Is it the fault of politicians that democratic debate is so often reduced to the level of 'soundbites' and slogans? Or is it only at this level that most of the electorate are willing or able to engage in political debate? In the twentieth century, the hope was that mass secondary education would produce a politically informed and engaged electorate. One might argue this has become an increasingly forlorn hope. On the evidence so far, Plato's Socrates would certainly consider it to be wholly misguided.

We shall return to Socrates' assessment of democracy in due course, including the view that it is not a critique at all. Recalling the explicit pretext for the animal analogy – namely, why philosophers turn out villains – Socrates contends that the philosophical nature stands little chance of surviving, since it is precisely the child who shows intellectual potential who will be groomed by family and fellow citizens to promote their political interests (494b). 'Such is the death and destruction of the finest natures,' Socrates laments, 'which are already rare enough, we say, quite apart from this' (495b). The few who survive are those who, for one reason or another – Socrates' protection by a divine sign is mentioned, along with exile and ill-health (496b–c) – manage to keep themselves to themselves, 'like someone taking shelter behind a wall when he is caught by a storm of driving dust and rain' (496d). In brief, a vicious circle operates: the just city can only become a reality if the philosopher-ruler comes to power, but contemporary society is such as to corrupt anyone with the potential to do so. Indeed, on the ethical reading, one might with Annas question how seriously Socrates takes the possibility of actualising the ideal city, given the number of variables involved, and the extended discussion of the overwhelming likelihood that the philosophical nature will be corrupted. By contrast, on the political reading one might answer that, for all his pessimism, Socrates ultimately insists it is not 'impossible' for a city to 'handle philosophy without being destroyed' (497d–499c). Adeimantus agrees that 'there only needs to be one . . . with a city which is obedient to him,' and on this basis Socrates considers the matter closed (502b).

Socrates' Account of the Good (502c–521b)

Socrates wishes to move the debate on to the 'course of study and way of life' that will prepare the philosophical nature to rule the city (502c–d). The discussion is in two parts. The first part concerns the nature of the good, knowledge of which the philosopher-ruler must possess. The second part concerns the formal structure of the education system in the just city (521b–541b).

Socrates begins by reiterating that the philosophical nature is itself a rarity, and that it is rarer still to find the individual who, in addition, 'is capable of enduring the most demanding [branches of study]' (503e–504a). Adeimantus enquires as to the identity of these hitherto unmentioned studies (504a). In reply, Socrates recalls the observation made during the discussion of the tripartite division of the soul at 435c–d that the fullest account of the nature of the soul was possible 'only after a long detour' (504b). The 'most demanding' studies are to be understood in this context, because the foregoing discussion of justice failed to address a matter of the utmost importance. Adeimantus waits to be told the identity of this oversight, though Socrates suspects him of playing dumb: 'you've often heard me say that the most important branch of study is the form or character of the good (*to agathon*) – that which just things and anything else must make use of if they are to be useful and beneficial' (505a). Socrates emphasises the fundamental nature of such knowledge: 'if we don't know it,' he insists, 'then however much we know about everything else, without that, as you are well aware, our knowledge will be of no more benefit to us than if we possessed something without the good' (505a–b).

This is evidently a significant moment in the dialogue. The contention is over the precise nature of that significance. Is what follows of a part with the preceding discussion of the just soul, supplementing and extending it? Or does it supersede the preceding discussion with what is effectively a new account? The reader's decision on this point has significant ramifications for how the dialogue as a whole is conceived, reflecting different conceptions of what Plato is attempting to achieve through the dialogue form. On the one hand, the idea that one account supersedes another in the *Republic* accords with a dialectical understanding of the dialogue form as a means of raising questions and drawing the reader into philosophical discourse. On the other hand, the conviction that Book VI continues the argument presented in Book IV accords with an understanding of the dialogue form as a means of explicating a certain philosophical thesis. Socrates' remarks at this point in the discussion potentially lend themselves to either interpretation.

As to the ensuing discussion, Socrates says Adeimantus is already 'well aware' of the importance of the good. Socrates' confidence on this point is explained after he has summarily dismissed two of the competing definitions of the good: the popular view that equates the good with pleasure, and the more sophisticated view that equates it with knowledge (505b–d). While there is disagreement about the identity of the good, Socrates observes, all agree that the good is the ultimate end of action. Adeimantus' awareness of the importance of the good reflects the soul's possession of a 'sort of divine intuition' that the good is something over and above individual perceptions of it. This is not the case with the just and the beautiful: many are content with the appearance of justice and beauty. Concerning the good, 'they want things that really *are* good; they all treat the appearance of it with contempt' (505d–e). Furthermore, Socrates insists, one cannot understand justice and beauty unless one has a prior understanding of the good. As a result, it is imperative the philosopher-ruler possesses knowledge of it (506a–b).

And yet, if the good is neither pleasure nor knowledge, then what is it? Socrates claims ignorance on this point, but in lieu of an account of the good itself, and at the risk of humiliating himself, he offers to speak of 'something that is the child of the good' (506b–e). This is the pretext for three analogies: the sun, the divided line and the cave. Before we examine them, it is instructive to reflect on Socrates' use of analogy in this context, for it raises important questions about the status of the discussion that follows.

Note that Socrates reverts to analogy because he is ignorant of 'what the good itself is'. This contrasts with the analogies of the ship and the animal, in which analogy is used to highlight certain facets of an object of experience, namely, a democratic society. In these examples, it is clear how one might challenge the veracity of the analogy, namely by querying whether a certain aspect of the analogy is an accurate reflection of experience (it is in these terms that we interrogated the analogies as assessments of democracy). However, matters are significantly different in respect of the good. Here the use of analogy is proposed on the grounds that the object of enquiry is unknown. In this regard, the rationale for resorting to analogy is more akin to the rationale for the city-soul analogy. There Socrates proposes an analogy between the individual and the city on the basis he does not know the nature of justice in the individual, but that it might be easier to identify if it is viewed on a larger scale in terms of justice in the city. This differs significantly from the use of analogy proposed in relation to the good. The fruits of the city-soul analogy are to be tested by seeing whether what is said of the city is corroborated by what is subsequently discovered of the individual soul. If it is not, Socrates says, a return to the city and a new beginning will have to be made. But there is no clear means of corroborating what the analogies of the sun, the line and the cave propose concerning the nature of the good. Socrates' situation is not that of the scientist, who uses analogy to explain something he understands, but which is beyond the ordinary mind; Socrates employs analogy because he does not understand the good himself. Consequently, what he says is speculative: he has no means of determining whether the children offered in lieu of the father are indeed in his likeness. Perhaps, as Annas suggests, Plato 'thinks they are not the kind of truth that can be argued for, but must be accepted in the light of other considerations and arguments taken as a whole' (Annas 1981: 242). Still, the danger is that Socrates' account disappears into a metaphysical fog. Perhaps unsurprisingly, in the ancient world Plato's account of the good became emblematic of difficult and abstruse doctrine in much the same way that 'string theory' and the like have in our own time. There exists a fragment of a Greek comedy in which a slave remarks 'I understand that less than I understand Plato's account of the good' (cited by Denyer 2007: 284). It is not a foregone conclusion that the reader in the twenty-first-century will fare much better.

(a) The Analogy of the Sun (507b–509c)
Socrates begins by recapitulating the distinction between the 'many beautiful things' and the 'beautiful itself', the former objects of sense experience, the latter an object of thought (507b). He then asks Glaucon to reflect on 'how much more extravagantly the creator of the senses has made the power of seeing and being seen than the other senses'. Whereas 'for hearing to hear, and sound to be heard',

no 'third thing' is required in addition to the hearer and the sound heard, the case is different for 'the faculty of sight, and the thing which is seen'. In order to see its object, the eye requires light, originating from the sun. The latter, Socrates specifies, 'is not sight, but it is the cause of sight and it can be seen *by* sight'. Thus, in the case of sight, a triangular relation exists between (1) the sun as the source of light/sight that enables (2) the eye to see (3) the object of sight (507c–508c).

Socrates designates this triangular relation the 'child of the good, which the good produced as its own analogue' (508c). For as the sun, the eye and the object of sight stand in relation to one another in the realm of sensory experience, so (1) the form of the good as the source of knowledge/knowing, (2) the intellect which is thereby enabled to know, and (3) the object of knowledge that is thereby known stand in relation to one another in the realm of intellectual experience. As the presence of light enables the eye to view an object clearly, similarly when the soul 'focuses upon what is illuminated by truth and by that which is, then it understands and knows what it sees'. But if it 'focuses on what is mingled with darkness, on what comes into being and is destroyed, then it resorts to opinion and is dimmed, as its opinions swing first one way and then another' (508c–e).

Crucially, while the form of the good, as the 'cause of knowledge and truth,' is known by one who understands it, yet it is other and 'still more beautiful than, knowledge and truth': as light and vision are 'sun-*like*' but not the sun itself, so 'knowledge and truth are good *like*' but not the good itself (509a). Further, as the sun is the source not only of light 'but also birth, growth and sustenance – though it is not itself birth or generation', so the good is the source not only of the knowledge of things but of their 'existence and their being . . . though the good is not being, but something far surpassing being in rank and power' (509b).

The reader may sense an air of religious mysticism hanging over the analogy of the sun: at 508a, there is Socrates' explicit reference to the sun as one of the 'heavenly gods', as was normal in Greek religious practice; and less explicitly, at 509a, Socrates alludes to the silence of religious rites when, in response to an interjection by Glaucon, he asks for quiet ('don't even mention the word,' he insists). To this list might also be added Socrates' description of the good as the 'something far surpassing being in rank and power' (or, as some translations have it, the 'being beyond being'). Indeed, in the Neoplatonic tradition – beginning with Plotinus in the third century and perpetuated into the twentieth century by figures such as Simone Weil – the sun analogy is integral to a theological Platonism according to which the form of the good is construed as God (see Plotinus 1991: 535–49; Weil 1957: 132–50). That said, Socrates is not arguing that the good can only be spoken of through analogy because it is otherwise ineffable, as some mystical philosophies would have it. While the good is beyond being, it is not beyond the range of human intellect: the good can be known. Nonetheless, the contrast with a scientific view of knowledge is marked. While science looks to causes in order to understand the universe, Socrates takes a teleological approach that looks to the purpose – the 'telos' – of the universe: the good to which all things are directed.

The last observation brings into view an aspect of the account of the good particularly contentious to those modern philosophers who accept G. E. Moore's account of the 'naturalistic fallacy'. One of the questions arising from the sun analogy is why it is necessary to possess knowledge of the good in order to know other forms. In order to understand beauty, Socrates argues, one needs to understand the purpose of beauty, and the latter is only provided by knowledge of the good. In modern terminology, a 'factual' account of the form of beauty does not constitute knowledge of it: one must possess an understanding of the purpose or good of beauty; that is to say, one must understand its 'value'. For Socrates fact and value are ontologically inseparable. On Moore's account, by contrast, this is to commit the 'naturalistic fallacy' by not observing the logical 'gap' between fact and value (or 'is' and 'ought'). Yet 'fallacy' or not – a debate beyond our present scope – it is important to understand that a version of ethical naturalism is at the heart of Socrates' account and has been from the very beginning. To dismiss it now is to dismiss the argument of the *Republic* in its entirety.

(b) The Analogy of the Divided Line (509c–511e)
Glaucon is impressed with the account so far, and urges Socrates to fill in 'even the smallest detail' (509c). The result is the divided line, one of the most difficult parts of the *Republic* to disentangle. It is not even clear it is an analogy, or again if it is only an analogy. In the

preceding discussion, the analogy between the sun and the good was clear, but what, precisely, is the divided line analogous to?

Socrates proceeds from Glaucon's agreement that there are 'two forms of things, the seen and the understood' (509d). He then asks Glaucon to imagine a line – for the purposes of explanation we shall conceive it as a vertical axis – divided by a horizontal axis into two unequal sections, the section above the horizontal – (1) – representing the realm of the understood, the section below it – (2) – representing the realm of the seen or visible. Although most figurative representations of the line assume that (1) is intended to be the larger division and (2) the smaller, this is not clearly indicated. Hence, whilst Plutarch – c. 100 AD – supposed that the manifold nature of the visible realm warrants the larger section, in the fifth century, Proclus argued the reverse on the grounds that the greater size of the section reflects the greater clarity of the intelligible realm (see Denyer 2007: 293). This aside, Socrates subsequently instructs that additional horizontal axes subdivide (1) and (2) in the same ratio as the original division. The result is a line with four divisions: the intellectual realm (1) made up of parts A and B, and the realm of sensory experience (2) made up of parts C and D. A stands in relation to B in the same ratio as C stands in relation to D, which is the same ratio as (1) stands in relation to (2). As progress is made up the line – D through to A – one moves by degree from the more to the less obscure (509d–e). For the moment, the purpose of the precise ratios between the different parts remains unclear.

Socrates proceeds to allocate different types of object to each subdivided part. To section D, the most obscure part of (2), are assigned 'images (*eikones*), by which I mean in the first place shadows, and in the second place reflections in water, or any dense, smooth, shiny surface'. To section C of the visible realm are assigned those objects the shadows and reflections of which are to be found in section D: 'the animals we see every day, the entire plant world, and the whole class of human artefacts'. So, in section D we find the shadow cast by the tree in section C. Socrates pauses to make an important observation concerning the nature of 'the relation between the likeness and the thing it is a likeness *of* ': it is, he says, 'equivalent to the relation between the object of opinion and the object of knowledge' (510a). In other words, the participatory relation envisaged between the form of beauty in (1) and the beautiful vase in (2) is modelled on the relation between the shadow cast by the tree and the tree itself. In section B, what were deemed 'originals' in section C – beautiful vases, for example, the shadows of which constitute images of them – are now in their turn treated by the soul as 'images'. In addition, we see the thinking behind the horizontal division of the line according to specific ratios. The ratio of D to C mirrors the ratio between (2) and (1), since just as the shadow is the image of the tree, so the object of opinion is the image of the object of knowledge. Thus conceived, the line is analogous in the same way as the sun is analogous: the relation between the sections above the original horizontal axis in the realm of the understood (1) is analogous to the sections below it in the visible world (2).

However, this conception of the divided line is complicated at 510b, when Socrates considers the realm of the understood in more detail. To this point, Socrates has focused on the different types of object populating the different sections on the line: shadows and reflections in D, and physical objects in C. But he now switches his attention from objects to the faculties of the soul that comprehend them. This shift highlights the complexity of the divided line. Most notably, the line is not only meant to illustrate an analogy between the sections above and below the original horizontal axis representing the intelligible and visible realms; in addition, those realms are placed on a continuous vertical axis – the original line – matching faculties of the soul on the one hand, with types of object on the other in the manner of the earlier discussion. Thus, the divided line would seem to be trying to accomplish two aims, one of which is read along the 'horizontal' axis separating (1) and (2) – 'above and below', so to speak – the other along the original 'vertical' line separating faculties from their corresponding objects ('left to right'). Depending on how the rest of Socrates' explication is interpreted, the divided line is either able to bear the burden of these two aims, or it collapses under their weight.

In section B, Socrates insists, the soul 'is compelled to work from assumptions [or hypotheses] proceeding to an end point, rather than back to an origin or first principle'. The latter characterises the activity of the soul in section A, where 'it goes from an assumption to an origin or first principle which is free from assumptions'. By further contrast with section B, the soul in section A is not reliant on images, 'but makes its way in the investigation using forms alone' (510b).

As well he might, Glaucon seeks clarification on this point, and Socrates tries again. Returning to section B, Socrates observes that, in geometry and arithmetic, certain assumptions are taken for granted (the nature of odd and even numbers, and the three types of angle are offered as examples). On the basis of these assumptions, he continues, mathematicians 'go through the rest of the argument' by steps, reaching 'that which they set out to investigate' (510c–d). For the purposes of elucidation, mathematicians refer in this process to 'visible' images, 'although they are not thinking about these, but about the things these images are of'. In short, the mathematician has in mind the idea of a square rather than the particular square drawn to guide his or her understanding (510d–e). Understood in these terms, geometry and arithmetic remain tied to the assumptions on which calculations are based, 'unable to move in an upward direction' (511a). As to section A, Socrates says, 'you must take me to mean what reason itself grasps . . . when it uses assumptions not as first principles, but as true "bases"' from which it then proceeds back to 'the origin or first principle of everything'. Reason then 'turns round and follows the things which follow from this first principle, and so makes its way down to an end-point'. In so doing, he adds, it makes use of 'pure forms' alone (511b–c). The activity of the soul in section A constitutes an advance on geometric and arithmetical thinking, for while the latter studies forms in isolation, the former conceives them in relation to one another, that is to say, in relation to the good. Glaucon illustrates his grasp of Socrates' account by summarising it, and Socrates concludes by enumerating the 'four conditions arising in the soul' as they correspond to the four sections of the line, proportionately more truthful as one proceeds from D through to A. Section D is the condition of 'conjecture' or illusion (*eikasia*), and section C is 'belief' (*pistis*), and both of these are the subdivisions of the visible realm. Section B is 'thinking' or mathematical reasoning (*dianoia*), and section A is 'understanding' or dialectic (*noesis*), and both of these are the subdivisions of the intelligible realm (511c–e).

Socrates' introduction of mathematical reasoning as preparatory to philosophical reasoning raises a number of questions. First of all, one might ask why mathematics in particular is allocated a privileged role in the journey to the knowledge of the good. Socrates argues that mathematics belongs above the line separating the visible and the intelligible because its truths are not based on sensory experience (odd and even numbers, and so on.) At the same time, mathematics remains preparatory to philosophy because of a number of limitations. First of all, it remains bound to images (though it recognises them as mere images: it does not confuse the number five with five chairs). And secondly, mathematics does not interrogate the assumptions or hypotheses on which it is based. Only dialectical understanding does this, leading the philosopher back to the first principle, and thereby an understanding of the form of the good at the summit of the line.

A further issue recalls the question of the compatibility of Socrates' dual aims in the divided line. If, in the first instance, the account of the line is an attempt to draw an analogy between the intelligible and the visible realms on the 'horizontal' division of the line, then in respect of the additional aim of the line when read along the 'vertical' line itself, a strict correspondence between the different objects and the faculties that comprehend them is required for the different aims to be met without one compromising the other. Most importantly, it requires a distinction between the objects of mathematical reasoning and the forms in (1) to mirror the distinction between the objects of conjecture and of belief in (2). According to one interpretation, this is precisely what Socrates provides: while there is no explicit reference to mathematical objects as a set of objects distinct from forms, it is implied when Glaucon says at 511d that thinking is a 'halfway house between opinion and understanding' (Denyer 2007: 305). The two aims of the divided line are compatible. Other interpretations, however, contend that there is no precedent for the sudden introduction of a set of mathematical objects that are neither physical objects nor fully-fledged forms. Indeed, it is argued that Socrates explicitly contradicts their existence at 510d–e when he says that mathematicians have in view 'the square itself, and the diagonal itself, not the diagonal they have drawn', suggesting mathematical objects are essentially forms (Annas 1981: 251). And yet, if the latter interpretation holds, then we are left without a separate object corresponding to the faculty of mathematical reasoning, and the analogy between the upper and lower realms breaks down. On this view, the divided line buckles under the burden of its own complexity.

(c) The Analogy of the Cave (514a–517c)

The discussion of the divided line marks the close of Book VI. At the beginning of Book VII, Socrates proceeds to the third analogy, the most famous passage in the *Republic*: the cave.

The most obvious effect of the transition from the line to the cave is to relocate the discussion of the good in a socio-political context that dramatises the journey up the line as a process of liberation and enlightenment. Accordingly, Socrates introduces the analogy in terms of 'the effect of education – or the lack of it – on our nature' (514a). He asks Glaucon to imagine a cave with a long entrance as wide as the cave itself, in which human beings dwell. There they have been since childhood, shackled such that they can only see the rear wall of the cave, unable even to turn their heads and look at one another. A fire burning behind and above them provides light (we are to imagine that the interior of the cave rises towards the entrance). A path runs between the fire and the shackled humans at an intermediate level, with a low wall running along its length, 'like the screen which hides people when they are giving a puppet show and above which they make the puppets appear' (514a–b). Behind the wall, on the side of the fire, a separate group of humans hold aloft 'all sorts of implements' in the manner of puppeteers, some accompanying their actions with noises, while others remain silent. Those shackled experience no more of each other or the implements carried by the second group of humans than what they see of the 'shadows cast by the fire on the wall of the cave in front of them' and hear of the sounds that accompany them. Since the prisoners have nothing with which to contrast these sights and sounds, they understand them not as shadows but as truth. It is, Glaucon remarks, a 'strange picture' of 'strange prisoners'. Socrates replies that it is not as fanciful as one might imagine: 'no more strange' indeed, 'than us' (515a–c).

We might ponder to whom Socrates' 'us' refers. At first glance, it appears that Socrates is describing a totalitarian system in which a ruling elite exercise complete control over the imprisoned masses. But if we take the 'us' to be 'us Athenians', then, as in the analogies of the ship and the animal, Socrates is alluding to a democratic system. By this interpretation, the individuals behind the wall correspond to the crew and are analogous to the political class, and the prisoners correspond to the manipulated captain and would represent the mass of the population. As such – and as in the analogies of the ship and the animal – we might once again criticise the representation of democracy as overstated. On the other hand, we might view the 'us' as a more general reference to 'us humans', and thereby to the 'human condition' *per se*. If so, then, as we shall see, other criticisms of the analogy might be levelled.

At 515c, Socrates asks Glaucon to imagine what would happen if 'nature brought this state of affairs to an end', and one of the captives were released and compelled to turn and walk towards the light. No longer able to make out the shadows on the wall, and confused by the sight of the objects now passing before him, Socrates suggests that 'he'd find all these things painful', and be unlikely to agree that he was closer to the truth. Indeed, 'wouldn't he believe the things he saw before to be more true than what was being pointed out to him now?' Given half a chance, it is agreed, the individual would be sure to return to his former state, and, since he was pained by the blinding light, it would be necessary to use force to bring him out into the sunlight (515c–516a). To overcome his sun blindness, the released prisoner would require time to acclimatise to his new surroundings, looking first at shadows, then 'reflections – of people and other things – in water', the objects themselves, and in turn 'the heavenly bodies and the heavens themselves' by night. Only subsequently would he be able cope with the light of day and gaze upon 'the sun itself', understanding that it 'caused the seasons and the years, which governed everything in the visible realm' (516a–c).

Socrates adds a final speculation. Suppose the released captive was reminded of the cave; he would surely pity his former fellows, no longer able to respect those who are esteemed for their ability to remember the sequence in which the shadows pass. Furthermore, suppose the prisoner returned; he would be sure to suffer from night blindness, just as once he was blinded by the sun, and look extremely foolish in his inability to distinguish the shadows on the wall of the cave. On account of his poor eyesight, the returning prisoner would be mocked by his former fellows, who would dismiss the prospect of leaving the cave as the height of foolishness. In fact, was anyone to attempt to compel those who remained in the cave to make the journey out of it, Socrates asks, 'if they could get their hands on him and kill him, wouldn't they do just that?' (516e–517a).

At 517b, Socrates makes it clear that the analogy of the cave is to be read in conjunction with the preceding analogies. The realm of sensory experience represents life within the cave, and the light of the fire within the cave represents the power of the sun. The path out of the cave represents 'the ascent of the soul to the realm of understanding', namely, the process of education culminating in the revelation of the form of the good. This knowledge is difficult to attain, Socrates adds, but when it is, 'the conclusion must be that [the good] turns out to be the cause of all that is right and good for everything . . . I further believe that anyone who is going to act wisely either in private life or in public life must have had a sight of this' (517b–c).

It is generally agreed Plato intends the cave to map onto the divided line as follows: the situation of the prisoners in the cave correlates to section D on the line; the freed prisoner able to view the shadows and the objects carried by the second group of individuals correlates to section C; the freed captive outside the cave, seeing shadows and reflections, correlates to section B; and the prisoner looking directly at objects outside the cave prior to staring directly at the sun, correlates to section A.

One interpretative question arises from the correlation of the prisoners' situation in the cave and section D on the divided line. For if we take at its word Socrates' observation that the situation of the prisoners in the cave is analogous to the human condition *per se* then, on the parallel with the analogy of the divided line, humans are mired in a state of conjecture and illusion, unable to distinguish between empirical objects and the images of them. Yet in the divided line it is clearly section C, rather than section D, that represents the ordinary cognitive state of human beings. The problem is potentially remedied by enlarging the cognitive state of conjecture to include not only shadows and reflections, but in addition all the received opinions on which our individual worldviews are based. For many, a particular attraction of this reading is that it lends an added relevance to the cave analogy in the twenty-first century, given our increased reliance on images relayed to us via not only print media and television but also the internet (see O'Hear 2006). Depending on one's perspective, it is an interpretation that is either uncannily prescient of the human condition in advanced capitalist societies, or that wildly exaggerates the extent to which individuals are manipulated in a democracy (and in the manner of the analogies of the ship and the animal). What is more, it is an interpretative remedy adopted at the expense of the parallel with the divided line.

A further problem arising from the attempt to map the line onto the cave concerns the existence of mathematical objects, though it applies only to those interpretations according to which mathematical objects are forms. For if so, then a problem arises given that, in the cave analogy, 'section B' is allocated its own particular object in the manner of the other sections. On this reading, we have another reason for arguing that the parallel between the analogies fails when it is examined too closely. Alternatively, one might wish to contend that the parallels are only intended to be approximate.

Why Does the Philosopher Return to the Cave? (517c–521b)

At 517c, Socrates remarks that knowledge of the good is necessary for a role in public life. It reminds us that the observations concerning the prisoner's return to the cave are not simply a speculative aside: the philosopher must return to the cave and rule. Yet in light of the further remark that the philosopher is sure to excite the hostility of the remaining prisoners, we might well ask why he or she should ever wish to return. Would not the newly minted philosopher be happier – if only to the extent of being eminently safer – if he or she retreated from the political life of the city and dedicated him or herself to the love of wisdom?

Socrates raises the matter in the following terms: 'it is no wonder,' he reflects, 'if those who have been to the upper world refuse to take an interest in everyday affairs, if their souls are constantly eager to spend their time in that upper region' (517c–d). Nor is it any wonder that philosophers look foolish when they return, given the intellectual night blindness that is sure to afflict them. Outlining his philosophy of education, Socrates declares that the true education of the soul is not like putting sight into blind eyes: one cannot 'put knowledge into souls where none was before'. Rather, it is like turning an eye that already possesses the capacity for sight away from the darkness and towards the light: the soul must turn 'away from what is coming to be' – that is to say, the realm of appearances – 'until it is able to bear the sight of what is', namely, the form of the good (518c). This requires careful nourishment, he reiterates, for while the capacity of the soul for rational reflection is innate, 'made of some more divine material', it is easily 'coerced into the service of evil' (518e–519b). That said, there must be a point at which education comes to an end. Left to their own devices, the educated 'will never act, because they think they have emigrated while still alive to the islands of the blest'. They will need to be reminded of their duty to rule, indeed compelled to 'come back down again to the prisoners . . . [and] share in their hardships and rewards' (519c–d).

Glaucon baulks at this, describing it as 'very unfair'. Socrates' response reiterates the point made to Adeimantus at 420b: 'the law does not exist for the exclusive benefit of one class in the city', but 'for the benefit of the city as a whole' (519e–520a). It will be just to compel philosophers to rule, and accepted by them as the task for which they have been prepared (520a–c). Indeed, the city governed by reluctant rulers 'will inevitably be the city which has the best and most stable government' (520d). We might ask how this could possibly be so: surely the best ruler possesses an enthusiastic dedication to the task? Socrates disagrees in an argument that recalls a point made as far back as 347b–d. Only those rulers who have experienced a way of life preferable to political governance – namely, the life of philosophical contemplation – will be just rulers, since having experienced the philosophical life they will not seek self-fulfilment through the attainment of political power; indeed, they will hold public office in contempt. Rulers eager to hold office inevitably compete for power, condemning the city to endless internecine strife. The just city requires rulers who hold themselves aloof from their task; only the philosopher will do. As Glaucon willingly concedes, 'there is no one better' (521a–b).

It is an ingenious argument that, viewed in isolation, might be said to contain a profound truth. However, viewed in the context of Socrates' broader concerns, it is deeply problematic. First, it seems to confirm the suspicion that the philosopher-ruler breaches the principle of specialisation. To overcome the problem of the single individual with two jobs, we suggested, Socrates has to show that the ability to rule emanates from the ability to philosophise, as though the two were in truth a single role. And this seems to be Socrates' purpose in the discussion of the philosopher's attributes. Yet the conclusion to the cave analogy seems to suggest otherwise: the philosopher is qualified to rule precisely because he sees the philosophical life as wholly distinct from the practical life of politics. The fear that the philosopher ruler epitomises the unjust individual would seem to be confirmed. As Pappas concedes from the perspective of the political reading, this raises a fundamental question regarding the coherence of Socrates' proposals (Pappas 2003: 123). By the same token, on the ethical reading it highlights the tension in Socrates' account between the practical and contemplative models of the philosopher. Which is the model for the just individual?

A further problem is that while Socrates' argument may explain why reluctant rulers are qualified to rule, it does not explain why they would necessarily feel motivated to do so. In Books II–IV, justice is recommended as in the individual's own interest, but here we have an instance in which Socrates concedes that the just life is not in the philosopher ruler's self-interest. Instead, it involves choosing a less happy life in place of what Socrates explicitly describes as a supremely happy one.

Numerous efforts have been made to extricate Socrates from this dilemma. One possibility is that the philosopher understands the imperative to return in relation to the vision of the good. In Annas' formulation, philosopher-rulers 'know what is just because they have the knowledge that is based on the form of the good. Their return is demanded by the justice that prescribes disinterestedly what is best for all'. On this account, the philosophers' motivation is very abstract: they take a wholly impersonal view of their interests and set aside the life of contemplation because their judgements are made 'in the light of the impersonal good'. Yet this begs the question of why the philosopher should wish to sacrifice himself in this manner ('why should *I* do what justice requires?'). Annas rejects the argument that philosopher-rulers would not perceive a conflict between justice and their own interest since they have been trained to understand them-selves as 'merely' parts of the whole: it 'only raises more urgently the question why in that case *I* should want to be a [philosopher-ruler]'. 'Justice,' she says – alluding to the demand made of Socrates at 367d – 'was to have been shown to be in *my* interests. But now it requires that I abstract completely from my interests' (Annas 1981: 268–9).

Annas' argument is a substantial one, yet one might contend that it is predicated on what, from Socrates' point of view, is a false premise. Annas assumes that to understand one's self as part of a whole is to be 'merely' a part, and that to stop caring about one's own happiness in what Annas terms 'a specially intimate way' – that is to say, as an atomistic individual – is to 'positively stop being human' (Annas 1981: 266–71). It might be argued that while this may reflect Annas' conception of the human – and her ethical approach to the dialogue – it does not reflect Socrates' view, and regardless of the offence to our humanist sensibilities, it is essential to recognise this if we are to understand the philosopher-ruler's motivation.

To this end, it is necessary to examine the philosophers' motivation not simply in relation to their crowning vision of the good, but their education in the forms as a whole. This line of argument recalls Socrates' repeated insistence that, in the just city, each individual is a link in the unity of the whole. It bears repetition in this relation, since in the light of the philosopher's education in the forms, it might be viewed as the political counterpart to the epistemological relation between the 'one' form and the 'many' particulars. Thus conceived, philosophers understand their particularity in relation to the one; that is to say, to the community as a whole. Specifically, philosophers understand their participation in the whole as an obligation to rule. As in the epistemological relation between the particular and the form in which it participates, philosophers understand it is only in their proper participation in the whole that their purpose is manifest. Consequently, philosopher-rulers do not understand the return to the cave to involve a personal loss or the means by which their humanity is surrendered and they become 'merely' parts of a whole. In other words, they do not equate acting in accordance with the good with acting impersonally and disinterestedly. On this view, rather, it is only on the philosophers' return to the cave that they fully realise themselves as human beings (see Sheppard 2004).

I shall mention one more problem that, on the political reading, is brought into sharp relief by the insistence that the philosopher return to the cave. It pursues the implications of the separation between the life of the contemplative philosopher and the life of the practical politician, and bears on the question with which the digression began: the prospects for the realisation of the just city. For we might question how the philosopher obtains the practical skills that are surely essential in order to survive the rough and tumble of political life, not least the rhetorical techniques required to convince the masses they are the right person to rule. Socrates, it might be argued, consistently elides this problem. In Book IV we are told that governors and governed 'will agree about who ought to rule' in the just city (431e). But when attention turns in Book V to the practical matter of how the just city might become a reality, discussion of how such agreement is reached is conspicuous by its absence. The problem is implicit in the analogy of the ship when we consider what would happen were the true navigator to assert a claim to the captaincy. There are, one might contend, few grounds for supposing he or she would be successful. The navigator would turn to the task wholly unequipped with the rhetorical skills of persuasion that would seem to be essential in order to obtain a hearing. It is difficult to conceive that the navigator would not require these additional skills; for one thing, the crew do not even believe the art of navigation exists.

Socrates disputes the matter, though the basis on which he does so is far from clear. At 499b, he suggests the populace may have to be 'compelled to obey' the philosopher-ruler. A little further on, the suggestion is that the philosopher-ruler's dominion will be recognised 'if instead of bullying [the masses] you are gentle with them, and try to remove their prejudice against learning and show them what you mean by philosophers' (499e–500a). The last of these would seem to be the only realistic alternative available to the navigator, but again we return to the problem of how the task is to be accomplished. The cave analogy only appears to compound the problem. As we have seen, Socrates makes the point that the philosopher will 'blunder and make a fool of himself' upon his return to the cave (517d). He maintains, of course, that the night blindness is only temporary: in time, the philosopher will become re-accustomed to the dark and 'see a thousand times better' than his former fellows (520e). But it is not the philosopher-ruler's sight – that is, his or her understanding of the good – which is at issue. Rather, it is the philosopher's ability to convince the prisoners of the clarity of their vision. It is difficult to deny Socrates' own suggestion that the more realistic possibility is 'they would kill him if they could lay hands on him'; after all, the philosopher challenges every conception the prisoners hold dear. Moreover, it might be argued that possession of the rhetorical tricks of the political trade is precluded by Socrates' account of the philosopher's education. According to the latter, all the philosopher requires to rule issues from his philosophical nature, to which rhetorical skills of manipulation are surely inimical. There is, for example, no suggestion in the following section that the philosopher is armed with these skills in the later course of his education. On this argument, it is little wonder that they are reluctant to return (see Sheppard 2004).

The Education of the Philosopher-ruler (521c–541b)

Socrates insisted that the philosopher-ruler requires knowledge of the good in order to rule. He now considers the philosopher suitably equipped, and turns to the second part of the question: 'how people like this are going to come into being' (521c). What follows is a detailed consideration that differs from the response to Adeimantus by describing the specific matter of the philosopher's educational programme.

Socrates asks what subject is most likely to 'act as a magnet to the soul, drawing it away from the world of becoming to the world of what is'. It must also, he adds, be of use to military men, given that the need that 'these young men of ours . . . be warrior-athletes' in accordance with Book III (see 403e–404a). It is neither physical nor musical education, since these are both about the inculcation of habit rather than knowledge, nor can it be the practical arts, dismissed as demeaning (see 475e, 495d–e). As anticipated in the analogy of the divided line, the subject they are looking for is mathematics (521d–522c). However, it is not currently used as 'the perfect instrument' for drawing students up the line (523a). Socrates proceeds to consider the different branches of mathematics and how each might be so used. He begins with arithmetic and number (522c), and continues with plane geometry (526c), solid geometry (528b), astronomy (528e), and harmonics (530d). In accordance with his claim to ignorance at 506c, Socrates insists he is unable to give a full account of the culminating stage in the philosopher's education: dialectic. We can nevertheless be certain it is only through dialectic that the form of the good is revealed (531d–534d).

In place of this account, they discuss the qualifications required for the educational programme they have outlined, and at what age the various stages should be undertaken. Socrates suggests children best learn arithmetic and geometry through play: 'we shouldn't present these subjects as a compulsory syllabus they have got to learn'. During late adolescence, physical education is pursued to the exclusion of all other study. At twenty years of age, the group of potential philosopher–rulers is reduced by selection to those who are given a structured education in mathematics and science, and then, at thirty, it is reduced again to those who are subsequently given an education in dialectic. 'You must use the power of dialectic as your yardstick to decide who is capable of giving up eyesight – and perception in general – and progressing, with the help of truth, to that which by itself is,' Socrates insists. Great care must be taken at this stage to ensure that the wrong sort of individual is not introduced to dialectic. It is the way to the good for those with a genuine love of wisdom. But in others it will create a habit of argument for argument's sake, leading philosophy into disrepute. At thirty-five, they are obliged to hold military command for the purpose of gaining practical experience, and at fifty they are led to knowledge of the good. They will spend much of their time in philosophical contemplation, but in groups will be obliged to take their turn ruling. They will finally depart this life, 'and live in the islands of the blest' (536b–540c).

Socrates concludes by reiterating his answer to the question with which the digression began: how the just city might become a reality. The answer, he suggests, is to 'send everyone in the city over the age of ten into the countryside'. There they can be educated in isolation from the corrupting influences of an imperfect society (541a). Glaucon has an answer to his question, first put at 471c, and they agree that the discussion of the just city and its corresponding individual is complete (541b).

Books VIII–X (543a–621d)

We have arrived at the concluding books of the *Republic* (VIII–X). At the beginning of Book VIII, Socrates declares at an end the 'digression' on the practicality of the just city (543c). Recall that Socrates is about to embark on an account of injustice to supplement the account of justice in Books II–IV, when Glaucon interrupts him (see 471c). In Book VIII, Socrates returns to his original task, and it occupies him for the duration of Books VIII and IX (543a–592b). Still he is not quite finished. In Book X, the dialogue revisits the topic of poetry, first considered in relation to the guardians' education in Books II and III (595a–608b). While it has the appearance of a dialogical appendix, what transpires is the foundational account of aesthetics in the Western philosophical tradition. To this Socrates adds a discussion of the immortality of the soul, and further reflections on the rewards of justice (608c–621d), before the dialogue finally draws to a close.

Injustice in the City and the Soul (543a–576b)

At the beginning of Book VIII, Socrates recapitulates the conclusions of Books IV and V regarding the nature of the just city (543a–c). Glaucon supplements Socrates' recollection, and in doing so makes a somewhat puzzling remark. 'You were saying you regarded the kind of city you had just described – and the individual who resembled it – as a good one,' Glaucon recalls, 'despite the fact that you apparently had an even finer city and individual to tell us about' (543d–544a). To what 'finer' or 'more beautiful' city is Glaucon referring? White perceives a cryptic reference to a 'city of disembodied souls', uncontaminated by the corporeal world of appearances, and thereby even finer than the just city of Book IV. But it is no more than a cryptic reference, White adds, and plays no part in the central argument of the *Republic* (White 1979: 206). However, those who tend toward a dialectical reading of the dialogue – 'dialectical' in the sense used in the introductory chapter, and not an allusion to Socrates' discussion of dialectic in relation to the divided line – suggest an alternative explanation. Rosen, for instance, contends that Glaucon is alluding to the 'more beautiful city' – the '*Kallipolis*' – of Books V–VII. In the discussion of mathematical education in Book VII, Rosen observes, Socrates refers to this beautiful city as belonging to Glaucon. In the remark at 543d–544a, Glaucon returns to Socrates 'the parentage of the city that Socrates has attributed to him' (Rosen 2005: 306).

I mention the contrast between White and Rosen on this point to illustrate how different approaches to Plato's use of the dialogue form result in different conceptions of the content of the *Republic*. If one looks to what Socrates alone says to determine what Plato would have us think, there is no explicit suggestion that Books V–VII have transformed the account of the just city. At the beginning of Book VIII, Socrates speaks of resuming the discussion left off in Book IV as though nothing said in the interim diverges from it: Books V–VII are indeed a 'digression' within a single extended argument rather than a point of transition in an evolving discussion. If, on the other hand, one approaches Plato's use of the dialogue form on the assumption that the author's meaning might be gleaned from all aspects of the drama – not least the words of 'minor' characters – then there is much greater scope to interpret Glaucon's remark at 543d–544a as an allusion to the transformation of the just city carried out in the course of the 'digression'.

Turning to the matter of injustice, Socrates suggests they proceed in a schematic fashion by considering the four types of unjust regime alluded to in Book IV in a descending 'scale of general approval' (544c). The first is initially identified with reference to the type of government found in Crete and Sparta (544c), but then a little further on as 'timocracy or timarchy' (545c). The second is named as oligarchy, the third as democracy, and the 'fourth and last diseased state of the city' as tyranny (544c–d). Recalling the methodological assumption on which the city-soul analogy was originally predicated, Socrates suggests the four cities will correspond with the four types of individual or soul that comprise them (544e–545a). Thus, it is proposed that each type of injustice is first considered in relation to the city, and subsequently the relevant soul (545b–c).

The attentive reader might already query the status of Socrates' proposed account: is it to comprise a speculative history of what is sure to befall the just city, based on Socrates' observations of existing regimes? Or is it to be a purely conceptual classification of the different types of unjust city and soul, from the least to the most unjust? Cross and Woosley argue that it is certainly not the former (Cross and Woosley 1964: 262–3). If it was, then it would reflect a simplistic – and, one might add, unduly pessimistic – philosophy of history according to which change is always the progression from the better to the worse. In response, any number of historical counter-examples might be cited. For example, in his own lifetime Plato witnessed Athens degenerate from democracy into tyranny – the Thirty – only for democracy to be restored. Having said that, it might be argued that much of the socio- and psychological interest of the account lies in reading Socrates' account as precisely an Edward Gibbon–like narrative of cultural 'decline and fall'. If it is conceived simply as an *a priori* classification of types of injustice – with the odd

reference to contemporary examples thrown in – then the account of
political change becomes largely irrelevant. As Pappas contends, 'we
lose any sense that Plato locates the characteristics of various cities in
specific material conditions' (Pappas 2003: 170).

There is also the issue of the continued reliance on the city-soul
analogy. On the political reading, the analogy remains 'an important
part in Plato's argument' (Pappas 2003: 170). Yet as the discussion
proceeds, it comes under increasing strain, most evidently when
Socrates discusses tyranny and the tyrant. In order for the tyrants to
be truly tyrannical, there cannot be too many of them in the tyrannical city when compared to the number who are being tyrannised.
However, if the former are in a minority, then they cannot be
described as the representative type, which the city-soul analogy
demands. On the ethical reading, by contrast, the analogy is not an
integral part of the argument, and so its collapse can be viewed with
relative equanimity. According to White, for example, 'it is important
to be aware that what Plato is ultimately aiming at here is an understanding of the individual soul', to which end the important contrast
is between the soul of the philosopher-ruler and the soul of the tyrant
(White 1979: 208). By this reckoning, the discussion is simply refo-
cusing on what has always been its overriding ethical preoccupation.

(a) Timocracy and the Timocratic Soul (545c–550c)

Socrates asks how the city begins the decline from its just state (545c).
That it will decline, he insists, is inevitable. Socrates does not make this
point in his own voice, so to speak. Instead he invokes the Muses – god-
desses of artistic expression to whom poets conventionally appeal for
inspiration – and asks what they would say (545c–e). (The reader may
wish to ponder the dramatic significance, if any, of the distance
Socrates places between himself and his words at this point.) Socrates
supposes that they would say something like ' "destruction awaits
everything that comes to be" ', adding that this applies to the just city
as to everything else. Wise though the philosopher rulers are, they are
sure to miscalculate in implementing the programme of breeding and
birth control: ' "success will elude them, and they will sometimes
produce children they should not produce" '. These children will in due
course come to power, despite lacking the requisite ability to rule, and
they will neglect the system of education. This will in turn produce

rulers even less suited to the task, and over time the ruling class will become thoroughly eroded (546a–547a). In short, the city will lose its reason.

A state of 'civil war' will result and two groups will emerge: one that 'draws the state towards commerce' in seeking satisfaction of its material desires, another that clings to 'virtue and the traditional order'. Their struggle will conclude in a compromise by the terms of which the city's property is divided between them – thus signalling the end of communal ownership – and the class of skilled workers is enslaved (547b–c). The resulting regime is described as a 'halfway house between aristocracy [the 'rule of the best' embodied in the just city] and oligarchy', and is characterised as a timocracy because of 'the value it places on military deceptions and stratagems, and the way it spends its entire time at war' (547e–548a). Born of conflict, in which the spirited part of the soul is inevitably dominant, its defining characteristic is 'love of victory and honour (*time*)'. This is its good aspect; its bad aspect is that, with the introduction of private property, individuals become increasingly avaricious, 'with a fierce and secret passion for gold and silver' (548a–c).

The timocratic individual is similarly located between the aristocrat and the oligarch. Socrates describes the fully formed timocrat before explaining how he degenerates from the aristocrat. Reflecting his intermediate nature, the timocrat loves the arts but is not properly educated in them; he loves good speeches but cannot make them himself; and his infatuation with power and glory means he is extremely deferential to those in authority, while at the same time he is extremely contemptuous of his slaves (the aristocrat, by contrast, simply holds himself aloof from the latter). The timocrat loves outdoor pursuits, and in accordance with his spirited nature believes he is qualified to rule 'because of his warlike deeds and achievements in war'. Lastly, he despises money as a youth but, as he ages, comes to covet it as a result of his fundamental lack of what, in the aristocratic individual, protects excellence from erosion, namely reason (548d–549b).

As to his origins, the timocrat arises from a situation where a good ruler – the timocrat's father – finds himself part of an ill-governed state. The father retreats from public life, and at home submits to his wife's incessant criticism, as a result of which his son views him as a coward. This view is reinforced by the opinions about his father that the son hears expressed in public, though he remains torn between his father's rational voice on the one hand, and the voice of those who criticise him, feeding the spirited and desiring parts of the soul, on the other. It is as such that he represents a 'halfway house', though in due course he becomes increasingly consumed by arrogance and ambition (549c–550b).

(b) Oligarchy and the Oligarchic Soul (550c–555b)

As reason cedes to spirit in the initial degeneration of the city and the soul, so spirit cedes to desire in the descent into oligarchy, specifically the desire for material wealth. Indeed, while oligarchy literally means 'the rule of the few', Socrates takes it to mean the rule of the rich minority; that is to say, those in whom the desire for money is dominant.

The origin of the oligarchic city is located in the timocrat's growing avarice. In due course, Socrates contends, the timocratic city will be 'destroyed by the strong room full of gold which each man possesses'. The process begins when the rulers in a timocracy bend existing laws to accommodate their desires, and it gathers momentum when they start competing with one another: 'in this way they would reduce the whole population to their own level'. As their avarice increases, so their commitment to excellence will diminish. In Socrates' words, 'as wealth and the wealthy are valued more in a city, so goodness and the good are valued less'. In particular, ambition for honour becomes transmuted into ambition for money: 'they praise and admire the rich man, and admit him to positions of power. The poor man they treat with contempt'. A wealth qualification is introduced, debarring anyone who does not own sufficient property from holding political office. As required, force will be used to ensure the population comply (550d–551b).

The most immediate limitation of the oligarchic regime, Socrates says, is embodied in its guiding principle: how much an individual owns is the truest indicator of his qualification to rule (551c). But there are others. The city would in truth be two cities: 'a city of the poor and a city of the rich', forever at each other's throats. This is one reason why the oligarchic city would be ineffective in war, since the ruling elite would fear arming the common people. In addition, the avaricious oligarchs would be unwilling to commit funds to defence (551d–e), and in any case the further erosion of the principle of specialisation would make it very difficult to maintain a standing army: 'the same people . . . are jacks of all trades and masters of none' (551e–552a). But the greatest evil that will afflict the oligarchy is individuals selling their property and remaining within the city, in effect removing themselves from one of the three classes (552a–b). In the city of vagrants that would result, even the rich individual is 'a blight on the city', since rather than fulfilling an important function he merely spends (552b–c). Still, the latter is like a drone without a sting, while the poor man is more likely to be 'from the class with stings', since where there are vagrants there are invariably other criminal types. The product of poor education and upbringing, those with stings will need to be controlled by force (552c–e).

Regarding the oligarchic soul, the discussion is again cast in terms of a son's reaction to his – in this instance, timarchic – father. The son first of all seeks to emulate his father, but then sees him taken to court for one reason or another and subsequently ruined. Disillusioned and poor, the son forswears any lingering attachment to honour and 'turns to making money', crowning the avaricious part of the soul as its 'great king' and reducing the spirited and rational parts to 'slavery' (553a–d). However, the victory of the desiring part of the soul leads not to psychic stability but to internal conflict, as different desires compete for supremacy. It is in these terms that the oligarchic soul mirrors the oligarchic city: as the city is two cities, so the oligarch is 'two individuals' with two sets of desires; those that are conducive to the accumulation of wealth, and those that are not. The desire for wealth only prevails if the latter set of desires is suppressed, with the result that the oligarch 'makes a comparatively good impression'. But the appearance is deceptive: it is not a rational commitment to the good that lies behind the oligarch's efforts to control himself, rather it is fear of losing his fortune. The oligarch is 'a sordid little fellow . . . a miser' (553e–555a).

(c) Democracy and the Democratic Soul (555b–562a)
Having degenerated in accordance with the hierarchy within the soul, reaching its nadir with the oligarchic supremacy of the desire for money, one might wonder what further depths the city has to plumb. As we have seen, however, a vestige of self-control is retained in the

oligarchic soul because of the need to maintain a good reputation in business. Thanks to it, Socrates suggests, 'for the most part his better desires have the upper hand over his worse desires' (554e). Ceding this remnant of excellence is key to understanding the further decline into the democratic city and soul.

Socrates is clear: the democratic city results from the oligarchic pre-occupation with 'the requirement to become as rich as possible' (555b). He describes a scenario in which the rulers of the oligarchy fail to insist on self-restraint among the young, since, from offering easy credit and buying up their property, the rulers see an opportunity to enrich themselves and consolidate their position (555c). In time the city will become increasingly full of indebted and/or disenfranchised individuals who 'sit around armed in the city' and nurse their grievances (555d). Meanwhile, the children of the rich are brought up to be 'incapable alike of physical and mental exertion, weak when it comes to resisting pleasure or pain, and lazy' (556b–c). Consequently, when rich and poor come into contact – in the context of military service, for example – the poor will say the ever more indolent rich are ' " ours for the plucking" ' (556c–e). The poor will rebel, and the city will become a democracy when the rich, either by threat or the actual use of violence, relinquish their stranglehold on the political life of the city (557a).

The result is 'a city full of freedom' in which the individual is at liberty to say and do whatever he or she wants, living whichever life best pleases them (557b). Thus conceived, it is 'probably the most attractive of the regimes'; it contains the most variety, and it is the regime within which all other types of regime are to be found. 'So anyone wanting to found a city . . . will probably find he has to go to a city with a democratic regime, and there choose whatever political arrangements he fancies, like shopping for constitutions within a bazaar' (557d). Indeed, the freedom on offer is such that there is no obligation to exercise any civil responsibility whatsoever. The individual is neither obliged to engage in public life nor obey the laws set down by those who do. A criminal can even ignore the sentence determined by the courts, 'without anyone caring or noticing', a reflection of the city's extreme tolerance (558a–b). 'You'd expect it to be an enjoyable kind of regime,' Socrates concludes, 'anarchic, colourful, and granting equality of a sort to equals and unequals alike'. Far from the rule of the best, 'all anyone has to do to win favour is to say he is a friend of the people' (558b–c).

As to the democratic individual, he grows up like his oligarchic father, mastering his 'unnecessary desires' in the name of thrift (558c–d). Socrates pauses to clarify the distinction between necessary and unnecessary desires. Necessary desires, he says, are those 'we can't deny' and 'contribute to some function' – the example of eating for one's health is offered – while unnecessary desires are those 'harmful to the body . . . and to the soul's capacity for thought and self-control' (the examples given are of extravagant eating and – less obviously – sex, presumably when it is pursued for pleasure alone) (558d–559c). The deterioration in the son's soul occurs when he falls into the wrong company and is encouraged to forego his father's self-restraint and indulge in 'pleasures of every kind, hue and variety' (559d–e). Torn between his father's example and that set by his new acquaintances, the latter ultimately prevails because the son does not possess the education required to give authoritative guidance. The appeal of his unnecessary desires wins out, though with age he may mellow and a certain balance between the necessary and the unnecessary may return. Still, the democrat mirrors the democratic regime's egalitarian embrace of every type of constitution by likewise 'putting all his pleasures on an equal footing'. Concerned exclusively with the 'pleasure of the moment', Socrates continues, no desire is overlooked: 'he rejects none of them, but gives sustenance to all alike' (559c–561b). At the mercy of his whims, one day the democrat gets drunk, the next he develops a passion for a healthy lifestyle; then he becomes indolent, before taking to philosophy and then to politics. In turn, he develops a passion for the military and for business. 'There is no controlling order or necessity in his life; as far as he is concerned, it is pleasant, free and blessed, and he sticks to it his whole life through', the envy of many (561c–e).

(d) Tyranny and the Tyrannical Soul (562a–576b)
Before reflecting on Socrates' critique of democracy – both as it is explicitly articulated in Book VIII and in the broader context of the ship and animal analogies – it is necessary to proceed with the account of tyranny for the further light it sheds on the matter. Not

that the discussion of tyranny is significant for this reason alone. As we shall see, it has a key role to play in the remaining discussion.

Socrates suggests that as the oligarchic city was undermined by its idealisation of money, so democracy is ultimately undermined by its ideal: freedom (562a–c). (Note that the timocratic city, by contrast, is not destroyed by an excessive attachment to honour.) There comes a point, Socrates predicts, when the thirst for freedom demands all hierarchical structures and systems of authority be dismantled. 'Praise and respect,' Socrates maintains, 'go to rulers for behaving like those they rule, and to those they rule for behaving like rulers' (562d). Similarly, fathers imitate their sons, and sons become accustomed to acting like their fathers; teachers 'are afraid of their pupils and curry favour with them'; 'the young are the image of their elders', and 'the old descend to the level of the young'. Socrates says the high-water mark is reached when slaves are 'every bit as free as those who bought them,' and women achieve legal and social equality with men. In an especially hyperbolic touch, Socrates adds that even animals become caught up in the egalitarian frenzy (562e–563d). It is a city in which the rule of law is ignored altogether, and each individual is extremely sensitive about any suggestion that they exercise self-restraint (563d–e). Anarchy rules.

Tyranny emerges from this state of affairs in a 'violent reaction in the opposite direction': from 'excessive freedom' the city lurches towards 'excessive slavery' (564a). Socrates distinguishes between three groups in the democratic city in a parody of the tripartite division in the just city: first the drones, recalled from the oligarchic city, who dominate the democratic city thanks to their 'talking and acting'; second, those disciplined few who accumulate riches, and on whom the drones feed; and third the general populace, the largest and potentially the most powerful class, 'but only when it is assembled together' (564b–565a). Conflict occurs when the drones assemble the populace to demand their 'share of the honey' from the rich, which they receive, though the drones retain most of it for themselves. To this end, the drones accuse the rich of acting like oligarchs, which they do in order to defend themselves. The reaction of the masses is to 'set up one single individual who is their own particular champion'. Having gained the support of the mob, the people's saviour disposes of those closest to him and requests a bodyguard for protection. His wish is granted, consolidating his position, and the tyrant is born (565a–566d).

Socrates then raises the issue of the 'happiness' of the tyrant and the city over which he presides. Initially, the tyrant is sure to be 'full of promises both to individuals and the state' (566d–e). But having dispensed with any internal challenges to his authority, he will have to initiate foreign wars 'so that the people will stand in need of a leader'. In due course, this will lead to fatigue among the populace, and those closest to the tyrant will become critical. Such critics will in their turn have to be removed, 'until he is left with no one who is any use', forever watching for anyone of ability who may become a threat. Contrary to the medical pursuit of health, which removes what is bad and retains what is best, the tyrant must execute the opposite manoeuvre. The tyranny is the complete inversion of the just city, which utilised all of the talent at its disposal lest it breach the principle of specialisation. The tyrannical city, by contrast, must destroy natural ability wherever and whenever it finds it. The situation escalates: the more hated the tyrant becomes, the more protection he will require, and in the end he will have to employ foreign drones and slaves to be those closest to him (566e–568a). Consequently, the population will find they have become ' " slaves to our own slaves " ', and regret the tyrant they have fathered. In the face of this growing resentment, the tyrannical son will have, in effect, to kill his own father in order to survive. The tyrant ends as the ultimate taboo figure: the – political – parricide (568d–569c).

At the beginning of Book IX, Socrates examines the character of the tyrannical soul and how it evolves from its democratic predecessor (571a). Socrates begins by recasting the earlier distinction between necessary and unnecessary desires. Among the latter, Socrates ventures, are 'violent or lawless' desires, emanating from 'the bestial, savage part' of the soul (they are often said to manifest themselves in dreams: 'attempting sexual intercourse with a mother' is mentioned). Such desires are 'stronger and more numerous' in some than in others. In the latter type of individual, 'under control of the laws and the better desires, allied with reason', they can be securely controlled, though not eliminated altogether (571a–572b). In the tyrannical individual, on the other hand, matters are different. Socrates recalls the democratic individual who rebels against the thriftiness of his father and indulges in 'excess of every kind'. Still he remains torn between the father and his lawless peers, and oscillates between the two. But the son of the democrat is thoroughly corrupted by those who encourage him to feed his desires, reaching the point at which lust (*eros*) has 'purged the soul of restraint and filled it with foreign madness'. In this way, *eros* – the tyrant within the soul – brings the tyrannical individual into being (572b–573c).

Thus, the tyrant is a slave to his own desires, his life an unquenchable round of debauchery in which each want is succeeded by another ('feasting and parties, celebrations and call-girls'). In time he runs out of money, and commits all manner of crimes to pay off his debts, including theft from his parents, if necessary by force. Any trace of decency is rubbed out, and his waking life becomes indistinguishable from what was once his dream life. When there are a large enough number of such individuals in a city, tyranny is born, with the soul most bloated by lust at their head. Prior to securing power, as private individuals they are either flattered by others or are themselves flatterers, doing whatever is necessary to fulfil their desires, at which point they move on. Friendship becomes impossible: 'they are always one man's master and another man's slave'. They are the epitome of injustice, the 'worst of men' (573b–576b).

(e) Assessing Socrates' Account of Democracy

The account of the descent of the city and the soul is complete, including, as we have seen, an explicit assessment of democracy to add to the implicit assessment contained in the analogies of the ship and the animal. In accordance with the terms of his original commitment to Glaucon and Adeimantus in Book II, Socrates now turns to the matter of whether the most unjust character will also be the unhappiest. Before following Socrates, however, we shall pause to survey the account of democracy in its entirety.

If it is difficult to draw simple parallels between democracy as it is described in Book VIII and Athenian democracy, then it is doubly difficult to see in Socrates' account straightforward similarities with our own situation. Nevertheless, the temptation to look for them is considerable, and not altogether misplaced. It might be argued that Socrates' democratic dystopia may yet return to haunt us, if it does not do so already. His vision of a fragmenting democratic culture united only by its capacity to consume, a culture in which the pursuit of the lowest common denominator has taken on the aura of a religious quest is not a vision we can so easily dismiss; there are too many signs to suggest it may already be upon us. Socrates' observation about fathers imitating their sons might be said to be a remarkably prescient case in point. Before the 'invention' of the teenager in the 1950s, the period of adolescence was understood as a time in which the young took on the attitudes and demeanour of their parents in preparation for adulthood. We might ponder whether we are currently witnessing the role reversal predicted by Socrates. Rather than the son imagining the day when he will be measured for his first suit, a walk down the average British high street would suggest it is now the father who dreams of owning the same 'trainers' as his son.

Still, on a number of points Socrates' account of democracy is hyperbolic and highly rhetorical, often lapsing into unrecognisable caricature. According to Socrates, the practice of democracy is largely indistinguishable from anarchy, for he cannot see how the line between liberty and licence can possibly be held in such a system (see 560e). However, from the perspective of a constitutional democracy founded on the rule of law, the answer to this problem is relatively straightforward. In the liberal state freedom is not absolute, as Socrates supposes, but qualified. As Mill insists, 'the only freedom that is worth the name is that of pursuing our own good in our own way, so long as we do not attempt to deprive others of theirs or impede their efforts to obtain it' (Mill 1992: 72). In other words, the individual is free to act as he or she wills until such time as the exercise of that freedom prevents other individuals from doing the same. The rule of law is fundamental in this respect, since it defines the limits on liberty that prevent freedom from descending into licence. The absence of the liberal conception of freedom in Socrates' account seriously compromises its effectiveness as an assessment of any democratic system we would recognise, it might be argued. Further, it is a good reason for challenging the subsequent explanation of the descent of democracy into tyranny. Socrates argues that tyranny results from an excessive desire for freedom. Yet as we discussed in the context of the analogy of the ship, in a constitutional democracy significant safeguards are put in place to prevent precisely this eventuality. Such safeguards are not an absolute guarantee against the fate to which Socrates condemns democracy, but they are certainly sufficient for us to question its purported inevitability (see Sheppard 2005).

Thus far, our assessment of Socrates' account of democracy has proceeded on the assumption that Socrates is fundamentally hostile to the democratic ideal. The nature of the just city and of the philosopher ruler, the analogies of the ship and the animal, and lastly the account of democracy as only one step from tyranny all clearly attest to this view, one might contend. Yet is it conceivable that the assumption is misplaced? Is it possible that, distinct from a polemic against it, Socrates' account is in fact a *defence* of democracy?

I suggested earlier there is an alternative interpretative possibility – associated with Strauss and Bloom – for those readers who agree the *Republic* is self-evidently a work of political philosophy, but who also incline to Waterfield's contention that, as such, it is wholly unconvincing. In the light of Book XIII, it is now possible to bring this interpretative possibility into view. The *Republic* is indeed a dialogue in which a totalitarian system of government is outlined, it is argued, but in doing so the author's purpose is ultimately ironic: Plato's aim is to highlight the preposterousness of the just city. It is Plato's intention, Strauss maintains, for us to conclude that the just city is 'impossible because it is against nature' (among others, Strauss offers the example of the proposals for the equality of the sexes and the abolition of private property). The *Republic*, in short, 'conveys the broadest and deepest analysis of political idealism ever made' (Strauss 1964: 127). Bloom makes a similar point in relation to the insistence that the philosopher has a duty to return to the cave. In the observation that violence may have to be used in order to ensure the compliance of the philosopher-rulers, Bloom argues, Plato points to the fundamentally unjust nature of the just city. 'This is injustice in the fullest sense of the word,' he writes: 'it would be contrary to their good to return. Or to put it into the formula for justice: the city would force one man to do two jobs, to be both philosopher and king' (Bloom 1991: 407).

In the event, it is only in the democratic city that the philosopher can exist. As Strauss observes, 'democracy is the only regime other than the best [and the best is impossible] in which the philosopher can lead his peculiar way of life without being disturbed'. The argument recalls Socrates' observation at 557b–d that the democratic city is the city 'full of freedom', 'containing every type of constitution in it'. Consequently, it is the *only* city in which the philosopher can live. As Bloom has it, Socrates 'is actually engaged in a defence of democracy against its enemies . . . After showing the impossibility . . . of a regime to which he could be dedicated, he progressively abandons it in favour of the regime which leaves him free, the only regime in which he can prosper' (Bloom 1991: 409–10).

The 'Straussian' reading – by which I mean to include Bloom's development of Strauss' position – has prompted a great deal of vigorous debate, though it is often ignored altogether in introductions to the *Republic*. Sayers is an exception, though he gives it short shift and is thoroughly scathing. The argument that the *Republic* is 'an ironic picture of an absurd and unrealisable situation' is itself dismissed as 'absurd'. Sayers is in no doubt that 'Plato believes in the ideal of a rationally ordered society. It is not a mere prayer or dream for him – he is a utopian social thinker. It is Bloom, not Plato, who rejects this ideal' (Sayers 1999: 130). In sum, to argue that Socrates fails to provide a satisfactory argument for how the just city might be actualised is one thing; to suggest Plato intended the gap between the ideal and the actual to be viewed as evidence of a critique of political idealism is something else altogether, and wildly improbable, it is claimed.

Sayers' reply will persuade many readers, suspecting that the Straussian reading is more a reflection of the liberal democratic concerns of our own age than an accurate assessment of Plato's intentions. Nonetheless, the debate begs an important question that a political reading like that of Sayers has to address regarding the relevance of the *Republic* in the twenty-first century. Given the broadly authoritarian character of the just city, one might ask why we should continue to view the dialogue as such an important contribution to political philosophy when it is so estranged from our own situation. It is a point made in a broader context by the American philosopher Richard Rorty. Rorty suggests of Plato's dialogues in general that they are obsolete texts that have lost their power to transform us in the twenty-first century (see Rorty 1998). It is an argument we ought not to dismiss out of hand, and to which the defender of the *Republic*'s pride of place in the philosophical curriculum needs to have an answer. In respect of the account of democracy in the *Republic*, one possibility is that the dialogue is neither an explicit polemic against democracy nor an implicit defence of it. S. Sara Monoson argues that Plato finds democracy 'repulsive and fascinating, troubling and intriguing'. Reading 557c, where Socrates makes the point that democracy is 'probably the most attractive of regimes . . . this regime will catch the eye with its infinite variety of moral decoration', Monoson contends that 'democracy's loveliness is not simply deceptive, distracting, and generally problem creating, though it is that. It is also potentially a resource' (Monoson 2000: 224–5). Viewed in these terms, Plato's attitude is perhaps not so different from our own.

The Happiness of the Just Individual (576b–592b)

We shall rejoin Socrates' discussion of happiness in Book IX. Viewed in the context of the challenge set to Socrates by Glaucon and Adeimantus at the beginning of Book II, we have arrived at the climax of the dialogue. Having established – to his own satisfaction at least – that justice is superior to injustice, Socrates must also show that the just man is happier than the unjust man. Glaucon once again replaces Adeimantus, and stands as Socrates' interlocutor for the remainder of the dialogue (576b). Three 'proofs' are then offered to establish that the tyrant is the unhappiest of individuals.

(a) Socrates' First Proof (576b–580d)

The first is very much a continuation of the account of tyranny – Socrates introduced the issue of happiness at 566d – and peers into the tyrannical soul to contrast what is to be found there with the just soul (at this point the city-soul analogy becomes very fragile indeed, as Socrates moves freely between the tyrannical city, the tyrannical soul, and the tyrannical ruler). The tyranny and the just city, Socrates asserts, are opposites: as one is the worst and the other is the best, so one is the unhappiest and the other is the happiest; and as for the city, so for the individual soul (576d–577a). Though the tyrannical soul may appear fulfilled, once stripped of its 'theatrical props and costumes', a different picture emerges (577a–c). In the first instance, while the tyrannical soul may appear to be free, it is in truth a slave, tyrannised by its own appetites: 'despite itself, it will be forever driven onward by the gadfly of desire, and filled with confusion and dissatisfaction' (577e). As a result, while the tyrannical soul might appear to be rich, it is in fact as poor as the tyrannical city, for it can never satiate its lusts (577e–578a).

Likewise, the tyrannical city and soul are consumed by fear. To make the point, Socrates focuses on neither the city nor the private tyrannical soul but on the tyrannical ruler himself (578a–c). In his own home, the private tyrant can feel relatively secure with his slaves, since he can rely on the city to protect him (578d). But what if such an individual were to be transported into a 'deserted place' where there was no state apparatus to come to his aid? 'Can you imagine the terrible fear he would feel for himself, his wife – fear that they would all be killed by his slaves?' (578e). And what if he were subsequently surrounded by neighbours who resented his mastery over others? 'He would be in all kinds of trouble,' Glaucon replies, 'surrounded and besieged entirely by enemies' (579a–b). This public imprisonment is precisely the situation in which the tyrannical ruler finds himself, Socrates contends. 'It's like someone having some physical ailment which stops his body being in control of itself, and yet not allowed to live quietly at home, but being required to spend his whole life in com-petition and conflict with other bodies' (579c–d). It is an arresting image, describing what we would surely consider a form of insanity and, contrary to Thrasymachus' original argument that injustice is the means to happiness, as 'utterly wretched' as Socrates suggests (579c–d). Well might we wonder with Annas whether such an indi-vidual would last more than a week (see Annas 1981: 304).

(b) Socrates' Second Proof (580d–583a)
If the first proof peers into the soul of the tyrannical soul, then the second and third proofs focus on the soul of the philosopher. Socrates begins by making an important distinction between three forms of pleasures, each proper to a different part of the soul; 'likewise three forms of desire, and three forms of rule' (580d). The desiring part of the soul takes pleasure in a diversity of aims, but is characterised in terms of its passion for money, 'because money is the principal means of satisfying these desires'. Hence, its pleasure is found in profit (580e–581a). Likewise, the spirited and rational parts of the soul take pleasure in what they each desire, the former 'a lover of victory and the lover of honour', and the latter a 'lover of learning and a lover of wisdom' (581b). Were we to consult the oligarch, the timocrat and the

philosopher, each would claim the pleasure in which they found greatest satisfaction constituted the greatest of lives. But which of them would be right? It is agreed that the matter must be decided by 'experience, reflection and reasoning' (581c–582a). On this basis, and in an argument that anticipates Mill's defence of 'higher' over 'lower' pleasures in *Utilitarianism* (see Mill 1992: 117–36), Socrates contends that only the philosopher has experience of all three types of pleasure; he is the only one 'whose experience has been accompanied by reflection', and by virtue of his powers of reasoning it is his reflective judgement that is likely to be the 'truest recommendation' (582a–e). Thus, the philosopher's judgement that intellectual pleasures are the greatest decides the matter of which life is the most enjoyable (583a).

Socrates' argument might be challenged on a number of points. Most prominently, there are the problems arising from the sudden introduction of pleasure to a discussion in which it has hitherto played no part. Pleasure is a wholly subjective feeling, one might argue, and so the attempt to rank objectively the pleasures experienced by different types of individuals is sure to founder, and with it Socrates' proof. Yet clearly Socrates would reject the premise that pleasure is simply a subjective feeling. As Annas observes, this rejection does not entail Socrates having to deny that the timocrat and the oligarch enjoy their lives as much as they claim, only that their insistence does not in itself establish the superiority of their life over the life of the philosopher. 'For a life to be properly called pleasant more is required than just that someone who has never thought very much about it, or experienced alternatives, should say . . . that he enjoys it' (Annas 1981: 308). If one has the ability to reflect on the matter, and does so on the basis of having experienced alternatives, then, Socrates argues, it is possible to arrive at an objective judgement, a point he will pursue in the third proof.

The introduction of pleasure aside, perhaps the most notable aspect of the second proof is the explicit allocation of a characteristic desire to each part of the soul. For if one shares the assumption that the dialogue explicates a single extended thesis concerning the nature of justice, one is now confronted with a significant inconsistency in Socrates' argument. On the face of it, one has either to insist that the notion of each part of the soul possessing its own desires was always implicit in Socrates' conception of the soul, or to concede the point. A good example of a commentator who wrestles with this dilemma is Pappas. Allocating a desire to each part of the soul, he maintains, 'significantly modifies the *Republic's* psychological theory, by adding a second feature to reason much different from its original characteristic of serving as an overseer to the whole soul' (Pappas 2003: 173). Socrates does so, he suggests, to make it easier to demonstrate both the philosophers' virtue and the rewards of reasonableness (see Pappas 2003: 197–8). Nonetheless, in so doing Socrates begs the question of the coherence of the argument as a whole (Pappas 2003: 197–201).

On the 'dialectical' approach, by contrast, there is no inconsistency by which to be troubled. Socrates' remarks on the desires of the respective parts of the soul are in keeping with the transformation of the account of the soul that has occurred as the dialogue has progressed, from an account of the rational part of the soul as purely calculative in Book IV, that is then supplanted in the course of the discussion of the philosopher – as the 'lover of wisdom' – in Books V–VII. Yet against the dialogical view, one might draw attention to the fact that Socrates himself repeatedly speaks as though he were advancing a single and continuous argument (the opening to Book VIII is an obvious example). In this difference of interpretation we again see the consequences of adopting different assumptions regarding Plato's use of the dialogue form. The latter criticism supposes that Socrates speaks for Plato; the 'dialectical' view, on the other hand, supposes that the author's intentions are not to be found in the words of one character, but in the dialogue conceived as a dramatic whole.

(c) Socrates' Third Proof (583b–587b)

The third proof, by far the most difficult to follow, is a further defence of the pleasures of the philosophical life, in the light of which we might, on the political reading, wonder what has happened to the centrepiece of the middle books of the dialogue: the philosopher as *ruler*. It might be suggested that the issues surrounding the single individual with two jobs has been solved by simply ignoring one of the jobs in question – ruling – and concentrating on the other, namely philosophising. Alternatively, on the ethical reading – and viewed in relation to Book IV – the third proof raises the question of the precise nature of the just life. Is it the life in which reason guarantees the harmonious ordering of the different parts of the soul found in Book IV (the 'practical' model of the philosopher)? Or is it the 'contemplative' model of the philosophical life that comes increasingly to the fore in Book IX? The final proof, it might be argued, serves only to highlight the tension between the two.

Socrates maintains 'for anyone other than the wise, [pleasure] is not true and pure, but a kind of shadow picture'. If this can be established, he adds, then it will be the most telling argument of the three (583b). Glaucon first of all agrees that pain is the opposite of pleasure, and that an intermediate state – 'a kind of rest or respite for the soul' – lies between the two (583c). Socrates then argues that what most people consider to be pleasant is only apparently so: 'what they praise most highly is the absence of pain . . . rather than any enjoyment'. In other words, they think they are experiencing pleasure when in truth they are merely experiencing the intermediate position of respite from pain (583d–e). Their ignorance is understandable, and arises from the fact that most bodily pleasures are of this kind, the result of the anticipation and cessation of pains such as thirst and hunger. Nonetheless, it remains the case that the majority of individuals are oblivious to the nature of true pleasure, which does not constitute a release from pain. Socrates offers the example of smell: 'you don't have to have felt pain beforehand', he observes (584a–585a).

In the next stage of the argument, Socrates builds on the point that most bodily pleasures are respite from a feeling of lack or 'emptiness', suggesting ignorance is 'likewise an empty condition of the soul'; as hunger is relieved by food, so ignorance is relieved by understanding (585b). However, understanding provides 'truer fulfilment', for it has the 'greater share in pure being'. Recalling the epistemological doctrine found in the middle books, Socrates asks Glaucon what he considers the greater: 'that which is connected with what is always the same, immortal and true [namely understanding] . . . or that which is connected with what is never the same, and mortal ['bread, drink, cooked food, and nourishment in general']? (585b–c). The objects of a philosopher's contemplation – the sources of his pleasure – are more real than 'the kind of things involved in the care of the body', will ensure the soul is more permanently filled, and are therefore the truer and the purer pleasure. The rest, by contrast, 'are like cattle, their gaze constantly directed downwards. Eyes on the ground – or on the table – they fatten themselves at pasture, and rut'. They are trapped in an endless cycle of desire and respite, since they fill their bodies rather than the part 'which truly is, the retentive part . . . *with* what truly is' (585d–586b). The tyrannical soul is the exemplary case of the latter type of individual, and as such the furthest removed from the philosopher. 'So the most unpleasant life . . . will be the tyrant's, and the most pleasant will be the king's' (587b).

Like its predecessor, this proof has attracted a good deal of critical attention. It is often remarked that its two stages sit uneasily together. While the first stage defines true pleasures as those that are not contingent on an experience of pain – on which account a physical pleasure such as smell might be cited as a real pleasure – the second stage deems all pleasures associated with the physical to be illusory; a strict division between pleasures of the body and of the soul is made, and the latter are associated exclusively with the intellect (see Annas 1981: 312). In addition, while in the first stage of the proof Socrates defines illusory pleasure as that which is in fact merely the alleviation of pain, in the second stage, true pleasure – that is to say, understanding – is defined in precisely the same terms as the alleviation of ignorance. As Pappas adds, moreover, 'nothing in the argument prepares for this claim, which feels like a gratuitous insistence on the pleasures of philosophy' (Pappas 2005: 175).

Pappas' observation recalls the point with which we began our consideration of the third proof, namely the identity of the just life and the tension between the practical and contemplative models of the philosopher. In the third proof, Socrates would appear to oscillate between the two. The first stage of the argument would seem to rely on the practical conception of the philosopher whom we see in Book IV, able to judge between all human pleasures, true and illusory, intellectual and non-intellectual; in Annas' formulation, 'the person who makes a just estimate of pleasures because he can take the rational view of his life as a whole and the lives of others' (Annas 1981: 311). However, in the second stage of the argument it is the contemplative conception of the philosopher that comes to the fore with the argument that physical pleasures are illusory and only the pleasures of contemplation are real. Still at the close of the argument, the practical model of the philosopher as overseer of the soul makes another entrance. If the entire soul is led by its rational part, then each part can fulfil its particular function 'and in particular each is able to enjoy pleasures which are its own, the best, and as far as possible truest' (586e–587a). Yet which of these two conceptions of the philosopher is Socrates' true ideal? As we have already suggested, in different ways this issue is pivotal to both political and ethical readings. From the perspective of the political reading, it is a question of the coherence of Socrates' argument that the just city can only be realised if philosophers become rulers. From the perspective of the ethical reading, on the other hand, it is a question of the precise identity of the just and thereby the happiest individual.

(d) The City in the Soul (587b–592b)

In the wake of the proofs, Socrates immediately turns to the question of '*how much* more unpleasant the tyrant's life is than the king's' (587b). There follows an arcane proof designed to establish that the just individual is 729 times happier than the tyrant (587c–588a). As White observes, how seriously the proof is intended is an 'open question' (White 1979: 233). Pappas is not alone in his belief that Socrates is simply 'playing with mathematics' (Pappas 2005: 176). Thus conceived, it attests to the Pythagorean fascination with numbers that runs throughout the middle and later parts of the dialogue.

The reply to Glaucon and Adeimantus concludes with specific reference to Glaucon's claim at 360c–362c that 'for anyone who was completely unjust, but had a reputation for justice, injustice was profitable' (588b). Socrates envisages the human soul as a composite of a 'many-headed beast', a lion and a human being, representing the desiring, spirited, and rational parts respectively (588c–e). To maintain that it is profitable to be unjust, Socrates continues, is like arguing that it pays to feed the many-headed beast and the lion while starving the human being, causing the beast and the lion to fight one another (588e–589a). By contrast, to maintain that justice is profitable is like arguing the 'inner human' should have control of the whole. 'He should make the lion's nature his ally, have a common care for all and tend all, making them friends with one another and with himself' (589a–b). However the matter is viewed, Socrates continues, it is obvious that the advocate of injustice is simply ignorant (589c–590a).

Socrates ends with the claim that the enlightened individual will concentrate not on amassing material wealth or honours, but on 'the regime within him', in other words, the city in the soul, 'and keep watch over that, being careful not to disturb any of the elements in it'. Such an individual will be willing to enter politics 'in the city that is his own. But in his native country, barring some heaven-sent piece of good fortune, perhaps not'. What Glaucon now refers to as the 'hypothetical city' they have constructed is, Socrates declares, a 'pattern or model laid up in heaven' for the individual who 'chooses to found a city within himself. It makes no difference whether it exists anywhere or ever will' (591e–592b).

It is interesting to observe how different approaches to the *Republic* treat Socrates' parting shot. For a political reading like that of Pappas, the reference to the city in the soul is dismissed as a now familiar 'disclaimer' that, while the ideal city may never be realised, it is valuable as a pattern for the individual to follow (Pappas 2005: 176). For the ethical reading, on the other hand, this passage is hugely significant as vindication of the view that justice in the individual has always remained Socrates' principal focus. As Annas puts it, 'politics and the management of society matter less than the individual and the personal struggle to be just' (Annas 1981: 320; see also Annas 1999: 81). In the final passage of Book IX, it is argued, the dialogue returns to its ethical source.

Socrates' Aesthetics (595a–608b)

The reader may well consider the conclusion to Book IX a good point at which to have brought the dialogue itself to a close. Regardless of whether one is completely convinced by his argument, Socrates has replied more or less in full to the challenge he was set at the beginning of Book II. What is more, the final exchanges of Book IX have about them the air of a carefully crafted denouement. Nevertheless, a seemingly indefatigable Socrates has something else to say about poetry. In particular, he wishes to return to 'our refusal to accept the imitative part of [poetry]' in the discussion of education in Books II–III (595a). Not that it is ever a question of retracting that refusal; on the contrary, in the light of the preceding discussion of the soul, Socrates wishes to develop the point (596b).

The argument possesses two strands, one in which Socrates develops a broadly epistemological critique of art, another in which he develops an ethical critique. They both lead to the conclusion that the vast majority of poets and their poetry must be excluded from the just city. Following Socrates' lead, we shall consider each in turn.

(a) The Epistemological Critique of Art (595b–602b)

Socrates maintains that imitative poetry is a destructive influence on the soul unless the individual exposed to it possesses an antidote: namely 'knowledge of what it really is' (595b). Socrates regrets having to say this, given the affection that he has felt for Homer since his childhood, but 'no man is worth more than the truth' (595c).

He begins by defining imitation (*mimesis*), suggesting they follow their 'usual procedure' of postulating 'a certain form . . . for each plurality of things to which we give the same name' (596a). The reader should pause at this proposal, for while reference to the forms is by now familiar, the means by which they are generated in the present context is not, and this has significant implications for the attempt to construct a 'theory of forms' from Socrates' remarks in the *Republic*.

Recall that the argument at 479a–e produces a form for every property predicated of an object in a qualified manner. It thereby yields forms that are perfect examples of properties, and it also restricts the scope of the forms. The present argument – following Aristotle, we shall call it the argument for the one over the many – seems to produce a form for each and every property that applies to a group of objects. It yields forms as universal terms, but it is not at all evident that these are perfect examples of properties, for while it is the case that for a plurality of things there must be a single form 'over' that plurality, it does not necessarily follow that the form possesses the property in a more exemplary manner. What is more, it seems to extend massively the scope of the forms, implying a form for each and every predicate, not least Socrates' own examples of couches and tables: 'when it comes to forms for these pieces of furniture, there are presumably two. A single form of a couch, and a single form of a table' (596a–b). In addition to manufactured objects, it also seems to commit Socrates to the existence of forms of negative terms. The predicate 'non-human', for example, applies to a number of things; according to the present argument, it follows there must be a form of non-human 'over' this plurality.

Other problems surface as Socrates continues. To the duality of the one over the many, Socrates adds a third: the maker of the couch and the table. Importantly, the craftsman is understood to have a mental eye on the appropriate form while he makes furniture (596b). Yet it is not at all clear how this can be reconciled with the preceding argument that the philosopher alone possesses knowledge of the forms. Further, Socrates will, in due course, speak of the form of the couch as having been 'the work of a god' (597b). But this in turn is difficult to reconcile with the claim in Book V that the forms are eternal, and thereby uncreated.

But let us return to Socrates' definition of imitation. He asks Glaucon to compare the maker of the couch with a 'craftsman' able to create the totality not just of earthly things, but also of everything in heaven and in Hades (596c). Glaucon imagines an astonishing individual, but Socrates suggests that in truth 'there's nothing very difficult about it' (596d), for he is speaking not of an omnipotent creator, rather of one whose activity can be replicated by holding up a mirror: 'that way you'll soon create the sun and the heavenly bodies, soon create the earth, soon create yourself', and so on (596d–e). Socrates is referring to 'the kind of craftsman a painter is'. Like the person who merely catches the reflection of an object in the mirror, the painter does not create a real couch, though he does create the appearance of a couch (596e). The result is a triumvirate of creators: the 'natural creator' or 'god' who makes the singular form of the couch; the carpenter 'who makes couches' with an eye on the form; and the painter, 'imitator of what these craftsmen make', who fabricates something 'two removes from nature'; an object not as it is but as it appears to be, a copy of a copy and thus a 'far cry from truth' (597b–598d).

This assessment of the painter is then applied to all other imitators, in particular to tragedians and their 'mentor' Homer, the traditional source of moral education who possess a reputation for knowing about 'everything human . . . and everything divine' (598d–e). The reputation is unwarranted, Socrates contends. If the tragedian genuinely possessed such knowledge, then he would not waste his time with images that are 'two removes from the real thing'. Instead of writing about the actions of others, he would be preoccupied with leaving his own actions to posterity (599a–b). Readers often observe that this remark displays an extraordinary aesthetic insensitivity on Socrates' part, at odds with what precedes it. Most notably, Socrates adopts beauty as his exemplary form in the middle books of the dialogue only to show himself seemingly ignorant of aesthetic value in Book X. It is somewhat incongruous, but it is to be borne in mind that Socrates' central concern here is the tragedian's claim to knowledge. No city has ever been governed better because of Homer's writings, he contends: no war has ever been won by his leadership; he is responsible for no invention; nor, in contrast with Pythagoras, has a ' " Homeric" way of life' been handed down to his successors. If the likes of Homer and Hesiod had possessed genuine knowledge of how life is best to be lived, rather than letting them 'roam the world giving recitations', their contemporaries would have 'grabbed hold of them as something more valuable than gold' (599d–600e). All artists are mere 'imitators of images of goodness and the other things they create, without having any grasp of the truth'. As the painter will paint the shoemaker without having any knowledge of shoemaking, so the poet uses words to bewitch his audience into believing that he knows of which he speaks. Inure oneself to his charms, however, and it is like looking at a face denuded of the youthful bloom that once made it so alluring (600e–601b).

Socrates makes a further addition to the argument, but it complicates as much as it clarifies in seeming to topple the craftsman from his new-found authority as one who knows the form. To the painter who paints the reins and bridle, and the leather worker and blacksmith who make them, Socrates adds the horseman who understands how to use them. The three individuals, representing three spheres of activity – imitating, making and using – correspond to a hierarchy of ways in which an object can be known. As the individual who understands the use of the object, the user possesses knowledge and can thereby issue authoritative instructions to the maker, who is thereby said to possess 'correct opinion' (601c–602a). Significantly, this condemns the imitator to what is in effect section D on the divided line, copying the craftsman without even 'correct opinion' about 'what makes any particular thing good or no good' (602a–c).

Socrates' estimation of the epistemological content of art will strike many readers as severely limited. It might be contested on a variety of points, depending on one's own theoretical view on the matter. From one perspective, Socrates' account is erroneous for restricting itself to a naïve representational model of art according to which the artist is no more than a copyist of a realm of appearances that is itself a copy, the artwork at two removes from the truth and thus relegated to section D on the divided line. In short, Socrates' argument simply does not apply to a good deal of what we might consider art (abstract art, conceptual art, and so on).

However, there are also substantial objections that might be levelled at Socrates if, following Aristotle, one accepts the guiding assumption that art is broadly imitative. By contrast with the study of history, Aristotle contends, which 'describes the thing which has been', art – the specific context of Aristotle's remarks is poetry, though the point is not restricted to it alone – represents 'the kind of thing that might happen'. Thus conceived, far from relegating it to section D, art is elevated to 'something more philosophic and of graver import than history, since its statements are of the nature of universals, whereas those of history are particulars'. That is to say, while history records the particular facts surrounding particular events, poetry makes universal statements in as much as it describes 'what such or such a kind of man will probably or necessarily say or do' (*Poetics*, 1451a–b). In sum, it has the potential to reveal universal truths about the human condition.

(b) The Ethical Critique of Art (602c–608b)

At 602c, Socrates shifts the focus of attention from the nature of the artwork to the moral effects it produces on an audience. Having established that imitation fails to reveal the truth of things, his aim now is to establish that its effects are inimical to reason and, as such, morally corrupting.

He is first of all concerned to establish the part of the soul to which art appeals. Our ability to see, he asserts, is easily misled. A stick that looks crooked in water is revealed to be straight when out of the water. The arts of *trompe l'oeil* and conjuring rely on this weakness to produce their effects. To combat them, the ability to measure, count and weigh is invaluable, for it enables us to judge which of our perceptions is correct. The latter is of course the function of the rational – and best – part of the soul. Consequently, if the re-invoked principle of conflict holds and it is impossible 'for one thing to have opposite opinions about the same things at the same time', then the part of the soul that is easily misled must be separate from the rational part. In other words, it must be 'one of the weaker elements in us' (602c–603a).

As for what is seen when one views a painting, the same is true for what is heard when one listens to a poet. The point is applied to poetry in an effort to show that imitation strengthens the weaker parts of the soul at the expense of the rational part (603b–c). Once again recalling the discussion of the soul in Book IV, Socrates reiterates that if a good man loses a son, he will cope with grief far better than anyone else. This is not to say that he would experience no pain at all, but that the exercise of reason would enable him to resist his grief by keeping the matter in perspective, thereby controlling the element of the soul that would otherwise indulge his sense of misfortune (603c–604d). The latter element, he continues, is 'highly susceptible to all sort of imitation', whereas the character in which reason holds sway is 'hard to imitate, and not a simple matter to understand if it is imitated', due to the public's unfamiliarity with such individuals (604d–e). Consequently, the imitative poet concerns himself with the 'fretful, variegated character' that capitulates to the lower element of the soul and dwells on its emotions 'because that is the one which is easy to imitate' (605a). As such, the poet is on a par with the painter: in his art he encourages the breakdown of the proper ordering of the soul by feeding its non-rational parts. 'By rights,' Socrates adds, 'we ought not to admit him into a city which is going to be well governed'; the imitative soul establishes a 'bad regime in the soul of each individual' (605a–c).

But it is one thing to corrupt the general public; the ability of imitative poetry to corrupt even good people is completely beyond the pale (605c). Even the best of us, Socrates warns, find it difficult not to succumb to speeches of lamentation when a tragic hero bewails his fate: 'we enjoy it, and surrender ourselves to it'. Yet when the good man suffers in ordinary life, it is 'the strength to remain silent, and endure' that we esteem (605d–e). Is it not unreasonable, then, to praise it on the stage? In the latter situation we believe 'there is a positive benefit, which is pleasure' in abandoning the rational to the non-rational parts of the soul, but Socrates fears the effects of taking such pleasure in the theatre cannot be restricted to it: what occurs there 'necessarily carries over' into ordinary life, feeding what ought by rights to be allowed to 'wither away' (606a–606d). Homer is undoubtedly the first among the poets, but it is also true that to live in accordance with poetry is to destroy reason. As a consequence, poetry is banished from the just city. Socrates acknowledges the 'long-standing antagonism between poetry and philosophy,' and says they will always be open to counter arguments, but if the individual 'is concerned about the regime within him', he will be wary of how beguiling poetry can be, and exercise appropriate caution (606e–608b). The implication is that in order to justify his admittance to the city, the poet will have to do so not through his habitual practice, but through philosophical argument.

Socrates' argument that art corrupts its audience through its use of aesthetic devices has had a long history, not least in religious critiques of art. In the wake of aesthetic modernism, however, the idea that only morally improving art is good art has become very unfashionable. For one thing, we no longer insist, as Socrates does, on the interrelation between the beautiful and the good. Where we do consider the moral effects of art, Socrates' argument is most likely to be contested along broadly Aristotelian lines. In the *Poetics*, Aristotle suggests that rather than threatening to destroy the order of the soul, the appeal of art to the emotions instead strengthens it. The concept of catharsis [*catharsis*] is central to this argument. When the expression of emotion is unchecked, Aristotle agrees it can be dangerous to the health of one's soul. Nonetheless, it is natural to experience emotion, and it requires some means of expression. It is here that aesthetic experience can play a role, for in the controlled environment of the theatre we can safely work through our emotions by empathising with a given character, subsequently returning to ordinary life with our mental balance restored. As Aristotle expresses it, tragedy contains 'incidents arousing pity and fear, wherewith to accomplish its catharsis of such emotions' (Aristotle, *Poetics*, 1449b).

A contemporary manifestation of the debate between Plato and Aristotle on this point is its contribution to the debate surrounding censorship, especially in relation to pornography and violent computer games. On the one hand, the broadly Platonic view is concerned that individuals, the rational parts of whose souls are not fully developed, may not be able to maintain a division between what happens on the computer screen and what happens in real life, and the psychological effects caused by what they witness on the computer screen will carry over into the rest of their lives. The effect of pornography on young men is often cited as a case in point. The argument runs that it is naïve to imagine that the way in which women are depicted in pornography will not, if the exposure is sustained, affect the view of women held by the one exposed to it. Therefore, access to pornography should be strictly controlled. The broadly Aristotelian view, on the other hand, maintains that, within certain limits, the opportunity afforded by pornography to purge one of certain sexual fantasies enables those desires to be safely channelled with a view to returning to everyday life in a fit mental state to develop healthy relationships. Therefore, pornography should be readily available.

The critique of art in Book X also raises issues pertaining to the dialogue as a whole. One issue that is often raised by first-time readers of the *Republic* concerns whether the author of the *Republic* would himself be turned away from the just city along with Homer. As a piece of mimetic drama, and therefore a copy of a copy, is the dialogue itself not twice removed from the truth? What is more, within the dialogue, can the same point not be made in relation to Socrates' repeated recourse to myths and analogies? How then does the *Republic* escape the censure placed on other forms of imitative art? One might cite the observation that the dialogue would be proscribed in the just city it describes as further evidence that we are meant to read the account of the just city ironically. However, many commentators – including Strauss (see Strauss 1964: 137) – mount various arguments for why the Platonic dialogue would escape the censure of the just city. Martha Nussbaum, for example, argues that whereas – on Socrates' account at least – the work of art seduces the audience into accepting the world through its appeal to the non-rational parts of the soul, the Platonic dialogue has the opposite effect, 'arousing [the soul] to rational activity . . . *motivating* an argument or enquiry' (Nussbaum 2001: 127). The same defence might be made of Socrates' use of analogies such as the sun, the line and the cave: their purpose is to stimulate philosophical reflection rather than to seduce us away from it. Thus distinguished from the imitative poetry to which Socrates refers, it might be argued, the Platonic dialogue can be admitted to the just city.

In Conclusion (608c–621d)

The dialogue nears its end. What remains is a discussion of the immortality of the soul followed by an enumeration of the rewards of justice to be had first in this life and then, in the light of a myth, in the afterlife. The overarching interpretative question in this section is whether it constitutes a fitting end to the dialogue. Is it, as Annas contends, 'lame and messy,' and at odds with what precedes it (Annas 1981: 353)? Or is it consistent with the original agreement that justice is valuable both for itself and for its – external – consequences, with Socrates now turning to a brief consideration of the latter? (See Pappas 2005: 188–92; Sayers 1999: 158–63.)

(a) The Immortality of the Soul and the Rewards of Justice (608c–614a)
Socrates' argument for the immortality of the soul proceeds on the grounds that, in considering the benefits of justice, we do well to recognise the brevity of our mortal as compared to our immortal existence (608c–d). He begins by securing Glaucon's agreement that there is a distinction between good and bad, that there is 'a bad and a good for each thing', and that the former is what destroys the latter; for example, disease is the evil that destroys the body (608d–609b). Socrates then suggests that if there is an existing thing whose particular evil is incapable of destroying it, then they will be justified in concluding that 'it was never in its nature to be destroyed' (609b). It is agreed that the evil of the soul is 'injustice, lack of discipline, cowardice [and] ignorance' (609c), but in addition that the presence of these evils in the soul cannot 'corrupt and decompose the soul until they bring it to the point of death, and separate it from the body' (609d). On the additional assumption that a thing can only be destroyed by its own evil – foreclosing the possibility that the soul can be destroyed by the evil that also destroys the body, namely disease – it follows that the soul must be immune to destruction, and hence immortal (609d–610c). Further, the number of immortal souls must be fixed, since they can neither come into nor pass out of being. If this were possible, then everything would be immortal, which is an absurd proposition (610e–611a).

Few would argue that this is the finest piece of philosophical argument in the *Republic*. It rests on a number of unsubstantiated assumptions, not least that for each thing there exists a single evil, and that the evil of the soul is the different forms of vice (injustice, and so on). Socrates relies on the notion that the good soul is the soul in which the parts are harmoniously ordered, yet it is precisely this assumption that he goes on to question in the passage that follows. The notion that the soul is 'highly variegated, or full of difference and inconsistency' is preposterous, Socrates insists, for this is impossible to reconcile with the notion of its perfection and thereby its immortality (611b). Yet, of course, the insistence on the simple nature of the soul would appear to conflict directly with the composite – specifically tripartite – conception of the soul that has been a feature of the discussion since Book IV. Socrates explains that in truth the soul is simple and perfect, as indicated by its love of wisdom, 'divine, immortal, and always existing'. At present, however, we are only capable of viewing it as a composite. The soul is compared to the sea divinity, Glaucus, whose original nature has come to be obscured by the shells and seaweed that have grown on him as a result of living in the sea (611c–612a).

Socrates' explanation has serious implications for the rest of the dialogue, if the reader chooses to dwell on them. It is noteworthy that in a political reading such as Pappas' reading, consideration of this passage is conspicuous by its absence. Sayers notes the 'drastic' nature of its implications, and insists the reader is faced with a choice between a contemplative and a practical ideal, arguing the latter reflects the 'true lesson of the *Republic*', namely that 'happiness can come only from the harmonious satisfaction of all parts of the personality', and not from focusing on the love of wisdom to the detriment of desires associated with the other parts of the soul (Sayers 1999: 160). But the issue is equally significant for the ethical reading in deciding which conception of the just individual we are supposed to take away from the *Republic*. Annas wishes to take away the practical ideal, and so she emphasises the point that the conclusion to Book IX corroborates this ('the justice of the just person . . . was the justice that required practical wisdom'). However, this means that Book X has to be marginalised, hence Annas' strategy of dismissing the whole of the final section of the dialogue as an unfortunate afterthought (Annas 1981: 346–7).

None of these questions seems to bother Socrates. Instead, he observes with some satisfaction that at no point in the argument has he had to 'resort to the rewards and reputation of justice' to substantiate his claim that justice is good in itself (612b). At the same time, there are significant rewards that justice brings to the soul. He suggests that the just man will receive benefits from the gods, who notice who is and is not just, and ensure the former are rewarded for their goodness, either during their life or in the afterlife, for they do not neglect those who seek to become like them (612e–613b). Further, the just man also receives benefits from his peers. Although the unjust may initially gain advantage, in due course they are usually found out, while the just men generally 'walk off with the prizes in the human realm' (613b–614a).

(b) The Myth of Er (614a–621d)

To end Socrates takes up the point that our mortal lives are merely a drop in the ocean of eternity. He relates what is known as the 'myth of Er', which explains what is coming to the just and the unjust human in the afterlife. It generally receives short shift in modern secular readings of the *Republic*, but it is a complex story that other epochs have found intriguing. In Ficino's *Platonic Theology*, for example, nearly half the references to the *Republic* as a whole are to the myth of Er. It tells of Er, a Pamphylian soldier who, presumed dead, led on the battlefield for ten days. On his funeral pyre, however, 'he came to life again', and had a story to tell of a vision of the underworld he had witnessed in the interim (614b).

Er tells that, upon dying, souls travel to a supernatural terminus where their moral rectitude is judged. The just are assigned an upward path to the heavens, bearing the mark of the judgement made of them; similarly branded, the unjust take a downward path (614c–d). Meanwhile, the soul sees others returning from their downward visit and others returning from their visit to the heavens. They have been in their respective places for a thousand years, and some tell of the horror, others of the bliss. Those who descended tell of the fate of tyrants and others who have committed the most heinous crimes and whose sentences are unlimited (614d–616a). Together these souls travel to another place, from which they are able to see the universe from a vantage point beyond it (616b–617b). At this point, the myth loses all resonance with the judgement stories associated with the Abrahamic religions but continues to bear comparison with Eastern religions that possess a notion of reincarnation, for it is to determine the nature of their next life that the gathered souls cast lots. This determines the order in which they are able to choose their next life from among the numerous available to them (617d–618b). Some make good choices, while others make poor ones, but it is emphasised that, apart from the element of luck contained in the order in which they choose – this may mean that a particularly attractive life is snatched before their turn arrives – each individual is responsible for the choice that he or she makes (619b–620d). The moral of the myth, with which Socrates ends, is that the soul is immortal and philosophy is the key to making good choices about how one is reincarnated; 'that way we shall be friends to ourselves and to the gods' (621b). The philosopher rules.

3. Study Aids

Glossary

The translation of certain Greek terms in the *Republic* is the subject of much debate, and in a number of instances has a significant impact on how a particular passage or theme in the dialogue is understood. The following list of transliterated Greek terms with alternative translations is provided in order to highlight some of the most important and contentious of them.

aistheton	Senses (as in sight, hearing, and so on).
andreia	Courage, literally 'manliness'; one of the four excellences possessed by the just city and individual.
arete	Excellence, virtue; that the possession of which enables the thing to fulfil its function.
dialektikon	Dialectic; the discursive pursuit of knowledge; more specifically, the final stage in the education of the philosopher, culminating in an understanding of the form of the good (and thereby associated with 'section A' on the divided line).
dianoia	Mathematical reasoning; thinking; deductive inference from premises; the cognitive state associated with 'section B' on the divided line.
dikaiosune	Justice, though not limited to notions of fairness and impartiality; hence some translations opt for 'morality' or 'the right'.
doxa	Opinion; associated with the visible or physical realm (the 'lower' part of the divided line).

dunamis	Capacity; power; ability; potentiality; that by which a being is able to carry out a certain activity or action (to see, to form opinions, and so on).
eidos	Form; idea; essence (when employed in relation to the 'theory of forms'); but also kind; type.
eikasia	Conjecture; illusion; imagination; the cognitive state associated with 'section D' on the divided line.
eikon	Image; the object of conjecture associated with 'section D' on the divided line.
elenchus	The process of refuting an interlocutor's views; a technique associated with the historical Socrates.
episteme	Understanding; knowledge; associated with the intelligible realm of understanding (and thereby knowledge of forms and the 'upper' part of the divided line).
epithumetikon	The desiring part of the soul.
epithumia	Desire; appetite; includes physiological, sexual and material desires.
ergon	Function; characteristic activity; work.
eros	Erotic love; consuming passion in general.
eudaimonia	Happiness; flourishing; fulfilment.
gennaios	Noble; grand; magnificent (as in the 'noble lie').
gnosis	Knowledge (as distinct from opinion).
gymnastike	Physical education.
hedone	Pleasure.
kakon	Bad; harmful; vicious.
kalon	Fine, noble, beautiful.
logistikon	The rational or reasoning part of the soul.
logos	Reason; rational argument or discourse.
meros	Part; element; constituent (as in the parts of the soul).
metechein	Participate; partake of; share; the term used to describe the relation between the intelligible and visible realms, the latter 'participating' in the former.
mimesis	Imitation; associated with the process of the artistic representation of the realm of sensory experience.

mousike	Musical and literary education.
noesis	Understanding; intelligence; pure thought; the term used for the cognitive state associated with 'section A' on the divided line.
nomos	Convention; law.
paradeigma	Model; pattern; ideal.
philia	Friendship; love.
philosophos	Philosopher; literally 'lover of wisdom'.
phusis	Nature.
pistis	Belief; conviction; received or folk wisdom; the cognitive state associated with 'section C' on the divided line.
polis	City; city-state; political community.
politeia	Republic (as in the longstanding English translation via the Latin translation, *res publica*); political system; the public and political life of the community ('political business').
psuche	Soul (as in the divine and immortal part of an individual); personality; self; psyche.
sophia	Wisdom; one of the four excellences possessed by the just city and individual.
sophistes	Sophist; literally 'purveyor of wisdom'.
sophrosune	Self control; self discipline; moderation; temperance; one of the four excellences possessed by the just city and individual.
techne	Skill; craft; art; an activity governed by specific rules and techniques.
thumoeides	The spirited part of the soul; includes indignation, anger, pride and self-regard.
thumos	Spirit; mettle; life force.
time	Honour; hence timarchy or timocracy.
to agathon	The good (as in 'form of the good').
to horeton	The physical or visible 'realm' of sensory experience; the 'world' of appearances.
to noeton	The intelligible 'realm'; the 'realm' of understanding or forms; the real 'world'.

Types of Question You will Encounter

The nature of the assignments you are likely to face on the *Republic* depends on a number of factors, not least the subject area in which you are studying it. Indeed, given that the *Republic* is studied in so many different disciplinary contexts – philosophy, political science, classics, psychology, literature and so on – it is imperative to acquaint yourself with the specific criteria by which your work will be assessed. What counts as an informed response to Plato in one disciplinary context, may not be quite so well received in another. This discrepancy is not necessarily to be ascribed to the idiosyncratic predilections of the individual lecturer or examination body responsible for setting the assignment, as many students like to suppose. Rather, it is because different subject areas are looking to assess different skills and understanding in different contexts. Nevertheless, your assignment is likely to take one – or a combination – of the following forms:

1. *Exposition*: you may be asked to explicate a certain passage in the dialogue – for example, the analogy of the divided line at 509c–511e – or a certain idea or theme, for example, the account of the forms. The aim is to assess your knowledge and understanding of the passage or theme by way of your ability to explain its content. In particular, you need to ensure that the key terms are identified, and the structure of the passage or the arguments employed is laid out in detail. In the example of the passage, you need to show awareness of the context in which it arises; and in the example of the idea or theme, select the relevant parts of the dialogue that need to be considered. Higher-level responses will also be able to identify important points of interpretative disagreement, and outline different suggestions for how they might be resolved.

2. *Compare and contrast*: you may be asked to compare the treatment of an idea, argument or theme in the *Republic* with its treatment in another work. Depending on the nature of the course, this might be a comparison between the treatment of the same theme in another work of Plato's – for example, you might be asked to compare and contrast the account of the soul in the *Republic* with the account in the *Phaedo* – or in the work of another philosopher; for example, you might be asked to compare the account of the philosopher-ruler with Hobbes' Leviathan.

3. *Critical evaluation of issues in Plato interpretation*: you may be asked to examine a contentious issue in Plato interpretation. For example, having been asked to explain the account of the forms, in the second part of the task you may be asked to assess its validity as a theory of knowledge. This type of task might also be appended to an assignment that begins with a 'compare and contrast' component. This requires not only that you are able to *explain* different perspectives on the issue, but also *assess* them with a view to arriving at a critically informed conclusion. In this connection, the judicious use of secondary sources is imperative. Ensure that you give a balanced account of the secondary sources to which you refer, and that your verdicts on them are reasoned.

4. *Critical evaluation of issues relating to specific subject areas:* you may be asked to relate the treatment of an idea, argument or theme in the *Republic*, to an issue in the subject area in relation to which Plato is being studied. In the context of a course in psychology, for example, you might be asked to critically evaluate how Freud would respond to Socrates' contention that the good life is the life of reason. Likewise, in the context of a political science course, you might be asked to critically evaluate Socrates' assessment of democracy in the light of the modern experience of democracy, and so on.

Common Assessment Criteria

As noted above, given the variety of disciplinary contexts in which the *Republic* is studied, it is essential to acquaint yourself with the subject-specific assessment criteria. However, the following criteria are more or less generic:

1. The ability to demonstrate knowledge and understanding of terms, passages, arguments or ideas.

2. The ability to select and appropriately apply that knowledge and understanding to specific interpretative contexts.

3. The ability to critically evaluate, showing the strengths and weaknesses in arguments and arriving at a conclusion germane to the preceding discussion. It is in relation to this criterion that the appropriate use of secondary sources is especially important.

Tips for Writing about Plato

Many of the tips that might be offered are predicated on specific methodological assumptions about the aims and purposes of Plato's employment of the dialogue form (see chapter 1: Introductory Questions). Thus, if one proceeds on the assumption that the *Republic* is a barely concealed treatise in which Socrates speaks for Plato, one might counsel against spending too much time worrying over the dramatic trappings of the dialogue, such as they are. Alternatively, if one resists this assumption, one might accordingly counsel against neglecting the possible ways in which the dramatic aspects of the dialogue impact on the course and content of the discussion. It is my hope that the following suggestions stand above the fray.

1. Whatever methodological assumptions you adopt regarding Plato's use of the dialogue form, and how, subsequently, the *Republic* ought to be read, be sure to adhere consistently to them. For example, if you begin on the implicit assumption that Socrates is not straightforwardly Plato's mouthpiece, making an interpretative decision that in some degree relies on this presupposition, then do not later switch to the practice of referring to Socrates as though he were Plato's proxy.

2. Having thoroughly acquainted yourself with the conventions for referencing Plato's works – as outlined at the beginning of the book – ensure they are scrupulously and consistently observed throughout your work. A badly constructed critical apparatus conveys a very poor impression to the person assessing your work.

3. Most readers will be studying the *Republic* in translation. It is important not to lose sight that one is reading a translation, and that certain Greek terms and phrases might be translated very differently, with significant implications for how a certain passage or theme is interpreted. Most importantly, you want to avoid a situation in which an interpretative claim you wish to make rests on the translation of a term or passage that, unbeknownst to you, might be translated very differently. This is to be borne in mind whenever one is working from a translation, but it is especially important when one is working from a text translated from ancient Greek, a language so distant and different from English.

4. Do not feel obliged to always quote the *Republic* directly. It is essential when a specific interpretative point is being made about a specific passage, but otherwise an appropriately referenced and accurate paraphrase will suffice.

5. When undertaking the critical assessment of an argument, concept or theme in the *Republic*, it is a good idea to first of all research whether or not Aristotle has something to say on the matter. If he did, then you are well advised to give serious consideration to it, for it is invariably of interest, and often a good first step in constructing a critical discussion. Be conscious, however, that Aristotle has his own purposes to serve when he speaks of Plato; he is far from a disinterested observer.

Bibliography and Guide to Further Reading

Plato's Works

The following are recommended translations of the *Republic*, to which Allan Bloom's translation is to be added (see 'Sources Cited in the Text').

Plato, *The Republic*, trans. Tom Griffith, ed. G. R. F. Ferrari (Cambridge: Cambridge University Press, 2000).

Plato, *Republic*, trans. G. M. A. Grube (rev. C. D. C. Reeve) (Indianapolis: Hackett, 1992).

The Republic of Plato, trans. Benjamin Jowett, 3rd edn (Oxford: The Clarendon Press, 1921).

Plato, *The Republic*, trans. Desmond Lee, rev. edn (Harmondsworth: Penguin, 2003).

Plato, *The Republic*, trans. Paul Shorey with parallel Greek text, 2 vols, The Loeb Classical Library (Cambridge, MA: Harvard University Press, 1935).

The following is a list of accessible complete editions of Plato's works:

Plato, *The Collected Dialogues*, ed. Edith Hamilton and Huntington Cairns (Princeton: Princeton University Press, 1989).

Plato, *Complete Works*, ed. D. S. Hutchison (Indianapolis: Hackett, 1997).

Further Reading

The following are monographs exclusively or in significant part concerned with the *Republic*, and edited collections of essays devoted to different aspects of the text. The reader is also directed to the books and essays listed in 'Sources Cited in the Text'.

Bernadette, Seth, *Socrates' Second Sailing: on Plato's Republic* (Chicago: The University of Chicago Press, 1989).

Craig, Leon Harold, *The War Lover: A Study of Plato's Republic* (Toronto: University of Toronto Press, 1994).

Ferrari, G. R. F. (ed.), *The Cambridge Companion to Plato's Republic* (Cambridge: Cambridge University Press, 2007).

Hyland, Drew A., *Finitude and Transcendence in the Platonic Dialogues* (Albany: State University of New York Press, 1995).

Kraut, Richard (ed.), *The Cambridge Companion to Plato* (Cambridge: Cambridge University Press, 1992).

Kraut, Richard (ed.), *Plato's Republic: Critical Essays* (Lanham: Rowman and Littlefield, 1997).

Murphy, N. R., *The Interpretation of Plato's Republic* (Oxford: Clarendon Press, 1951).

Nussbaum, Martha C., *The Fragility of Goodness: Luck and Ethics in Greek Tragedy and Philosophy*, 2nd edn (Cambridge: Cambridge University Press, 2001).

Ophir, Adi, *Plato's Invisible Cities: Discourse and Power in the Republic* (London: Routledge, 1991).

Ostenfeld, Erik Nis (ed.), *Essays on Plato's Republic* (Aarhus: Aarhus University Press, 1998).

Pradeau, Jean-François, *Plato and the City: A New Introduction to Plato's Political Thought*, trans. Janet Lloyd (Exeter: Exeter University Press, 2002).

Roochnik, David, *Beautiful City: The Dialectical Character of Plato's Republic* (Ithaca: Cornell University Press, 2003).

Santas, Gerasimos (ed.), *The Blackwell Guide to Plato's Republic* (Oxford: Blackwell, 2006).

Sesonske, Alexander (ed.), *Plato's Republic: Interpretation and Criticism* (Belmont, CA: Wadsworth, 1966).

The following are books and essays and books dealing with particular aspects of the *Republic*. They are listed in accordance with the part of the text to which they are most applicable.

Introductory Questions

Annas, Julia, *Plato: A Very Short Introduction* (Oxford: Oxford University Press, 2003).

Hyland, Drew, 'Why Plato Wrote Dialogues', in *Philosophy and Rhetoric* 1, no. 1 (1968).

Kahn, Charles H., 'Did Plato write Socrates' Dialogues?' in *Classical Quarterly* 31 (1981).

Lane, Melissa, *Plato's Progeny: How Plato and Socrates Still Captivate the Modern Mind* (London: Duckworth, 2001).

Moors, K., 'Plato's Use of Dialogue', in *Classical World* 72 (1978).

Nightingale, Andrea Wilson, *Genres in Dialogue: Plato and the Construct of Philosophy* (Cambridge: Cambridge University Press, 1995).

Press, Gerald A., *Who Speaks for Plato: Studies in Platonic Anonymity* (Lanham: Rowe and Littlefield, 2000).

Roberts, J. W., *City of Sokrates: and Introduction to Classical Athens*, 2nd edn (London: Routledge, 1998).

Shorey, Paul, *What Plato Said* (Chicago: The University of Chicago Press, 1933).

Taylor, C. C. W., *Socrates: A Very Short Introduction* (Oxford: Oxford University Press, 2003).

A Guide to the Text: Book I (327a–354c)

Barney, Rachel, 'Socrates' Refutation of Tharasymachus', in Santas (ed.) (2006).

Joseph, H. W. B., 'The Argument with Polemarchus', in Sesonske (ed.) (1966).

Santas, Gerasimos, 'Methods of Reasoning about Justice in Plato's *Republic*', in Santas (ed.) (2006).

Sparshott, Francis E., 'Socrates and Thrasymachus', in *The Monist* 50 (1966).

Sesonske, Alexander, 'Plato's Apology: *Republic* I', in Sesonske (ed.) (1966).

Thayer, H. S., 'Plato: The Theory and Language of Function', in Sesonske (ed.) (1966).

Weiss, Roslyn, 'Wise Guys and Smart Alecks in *Republic* 1 and 2', in Ferrari (ed.) (2007).

A Guide to the Text: Books II–V (357a–471c)

Blossner, Norbert, 'The City-Soul Analogy', in Ferrari (ed.) (2007).

Bluestone, N. H., *Women and the Ideal Society: Plato's Republic and Modern Myths of Gender* (Amherst: University of Massachusetts Press, 1987).

Hobbs, Angela, *Plato and the Hero: Courage, Manliness, and the Impersonal Good* (Cambridge: Cambridge University Press, 2000).

Lear, Jonathan, 'Inside and Outside the *Republic*', in Kraut (ed.) (1997).

Lorenz, Hendrik, 'The Analysis of the Soul in Plato's *Republic*', in Santas (ed.) (2006).

Morrison, Donald R., 'The Utopian Character of Plato's Ideal City', in Ferrari (ed.) (2007).

Saxonhouse, Arlene W., 'The Philosopher and the Female in the Political Thought of Plato', in Kraut (ed.) (1997).

Schofield, Malcolm, 'The Noble Lie', in Ferrari (ed.) (2007).

Shields, Christopher, 'Plato's Challenge: The Case Against Justice in *Republic* II', in Santas (ed.) (2006).

Singpurwalla, Rachel G. K., 'Plato's Defence of Plato in the *Republic*', in Santos (ed.) (2006).

Versenyi, L. G., 'Plato and His Liberal Opponents', in *Philosophy* 46 (1971).

A Guide to the Text: Books V–VII (471c–541b)

Bambrough, Renford, 'Plato's Political Analogies', in *Philosophy, Politics and Society*, ed. Peter Laslett (Oxford: Basil Blackwell, 1963).

Irigaray, Luce, 'Plato's Hystera', in *Speculum of the Other Woman*, trans. Gillian C. McGill (Ithaca, NY: Cornell University Press, 1985).

Kahn, Charles H., 'The Greek verb "be" and the Concept of Being', in *Foundations of Language* 2 (1966).

Keyt, David, 'Plato and the Ship of State', in Santas (ed.) (2006).

Lesser, H., 'Plato's Feminism', in *Philosophy* 54 (1979).

Mabbott, J. O., 'Is Plato's *Republic* Utilitarian?' in *Plato*, ed. Gregory Vlastos (Garden City, NJ: Doubleday, 1971).

Nehemas, Alexander, 'Plato on the Imperfection of the Sensible World', in *American Philosophical Quarterly* 12 (1975).

Nehemas, Alexander, 'Self-predication and Plato's Theory of Forms', in *American Philosophical Quarterly* 16 (1979).

Penner, Terry, 'The Forms in the *Republic*', in Santas (ed.) (2006).

Sedley, David, 'Philosophy, the Forms, and the Art of Ruling', in Ferrari (ed.) (2007).

Vlastos, Gregory, 'Degrees of Reality in Plato', in *New Essays on Plato and Aristotle*, edited by Renford Bambrough (London: Routledge and Kegan Paul, 1965).

A Guide to the Text: VIII–X (543a–621d)

Burnyeat, Miles, 'Art and Mimesis in Plato's *Republic*', in *London Review of Books* 20, no. 10 (1998).

Deleuze, Gilles, 'Plato and the Simulacrum', in *October* 27 (1983).

Gadamer, Hans-Georg, *Dialogue and Dialectic*, trans. P. Christopher Smith (New Haven, CT: Yale University Press, 1980).

Halliwell, Stephen, 'The Life-and-Death Journey of the Soul', in Ferrari (ed.) (2007).

Janaway, Christopher, *Images of Excellence: Plato's Critique of the Arts* (Oxford: Clarendon Press, 1995).

Moravcsik, J., and P. Temko (eds), *Plato on Beauty, Wisdom and the Arts* (Lanham: Rowman and Littlefield, 1982).

Moss, Jessica, 'What is Imitative Poetry and Why is it Bad?', in Ferrari (ed.) (2007).

Murdoch, Iris, *The Fire and the Sun: Why Plato Banished the Artists* (Oxford: Clarendon Press, 1977).

Parry, Richard D., 'The Unhappy Tyrant and the Craft of Inner Rule', in Ferrari (ed.) (2007).

Rosen, Stanley, *The Quarrel between Philosophy and Poetry: Studies in Ancient Thought* (London: Routledge, 1993).

Urmson, James O., 'Plato and the Poets', in Kraut (ed.) (1997).

Sources Cited in the Text

Annas, Julia, *An Introduction to Plato's Republic* (Oxford: Clarendon Press, 1981).

Annas, Julia, *Platonic Ethics, Old and New* (Cornell: Cornell University Press, 1999).

Annas, Julia, and Christopher Rowe *New Perspectives on Plato, Modern and Ancient* (Cambridge, MA: Harvard University Press, 2002).

Aristophanes, *The Acharians, The Clouds, Lysistrata*, trans. Alan H. Sommerstein (Harmondsworth: Penguin, 1973).

Aristotle, *The Complete Works*, the revised Oxford translation, ed. Jonathan Barnes, 2 vols (Princeton: Princeton University Press, 1984).

Berlin, Isaiah, *Four Essays on Liberty* (Oxford: Oxford University Press, 1969).

Blackburn, Simon, *Plato's Republic: A Biography* (London: Atlantic Books, 2006).

Bloom, Allan, *The Republic of Plato*, trans. with an interpretative essay, 2nd edn (New York: Basic Books, 1991).

Brann, Eva, *The Music of the Republic: Essays on Socrates' Conversations and Plato's Writings* (Philadelphia: Paul Dry, 2004).

Burnyeat, M. F., 'The Past in the Present: Plato as Educator in Nineteenth-Century Britain', *Philosophers on Education: Historical Perspectives*, ed. Amélie Oksenberg Rorty (London: Routledge, 1998).

Cross, R. C., and A. D. Woosley, *Plato's Republic: A Philosophical Commentary* (London: Macmillan, 1964).

Crossman, Richard, *Plato Today*, 2nd edn (London: Allen and Unwin, 1959).

Davidson, James, *Fishcakes and Courtesans: The Consuming Passions of Classical Athens* (London: Harper Collins, 1997).

Dante, *The Divine Comedy*, trans. Allen Mandelbaum (London: Everyman, 1995).

Denyer, Nicholas, 'Sun and Line: The Role of the Good', in Ferrari (ed.) (2007).

Ferrari, G. R. F. (ed.), Plato, *The Republic*, trans. Tom Griffith (Cambridge: Cambridge University Press, 2000).

Ferrari, G. R. F., *City and Soul in Plato's Republic* (Chicago: The University of Chicago Press, 2005).

Ficino, Marsilio, *Platonic Theology*, trans. Michael J. B. Allen with John Warden, 6 vols, The I Tatti Renaissance Library (Cambridge, MA: Harvard University Press, 2001–6).

Griswold, Charles L., *Platonic Writings, Platonic Readings* (London: Routledge, 1988).

Grote, George, *Plato and Other Companions of Sokrates*, 4 vols (New York: Burt Franklin, 1973).

Heidegger, Martin, *Nietzsche*, trans. Joan Stambaugh, David Farrell Krell and Frank A. Capuzzi, ed. David Farrell Krell, 2 vols (San Francisco: Harper Collins, 1991).

Hobbes, Thomas, *Leviathan*, ed. Richard Tuck (Cambridge: Cambridge University Press, 1996).

Homer, *Odyssey*, trans. Robert Fagles (New York: Viking, 1996).

Hume, David, *A Treatise of Human Nature* (Oxford: Clarendon Press, 1988).

Irwin, Terence, *Plato's Moral Theory: The Early and Middle Dialogues* (Oxford: Clarendon Press, 1977).

Kraut, Richard, 'The Defence of Justice in Plato's *Republic*', in Kraut (ed.) (1992a).

Kraut, Richard, 'Introduction to the Study of Plato', in Kraut (ed.) (1992b).

Mill, J. S., *On Liberty and Utilitarianism* (London: Everyman, 1992).

Monoson, Sara S., *Plato's Democratic Entanglements: Athenian Politics and the Practice of Philosophy* (Princeton: Princeton University Press, 2000).

Moore, G. E., *Principa Ethica* (Cambridge: Cambridge University Press, 1903).

Nietzsche, Friedrich, *Twilight of the Idols and the Anti-Christ*, trans. R. J. Hollingdale (Harmondsworth: Penguin, 1990).

Pappas, Nickolas, *Plato and the Republic* (London: Routledge, 2003).

Plotinus, *The Enneads*, trans. Stephen Mackenna, abridged John Dillon (Harmondsworth: Penguin, 1991).

Popper, Karl, *The Open Society and Its Enemies. Volume One: The Spell of Plato* (London: Routledge, 1995).

Reeve, C. D. C., *Philosopher-Kings: The Argument of Plato's Republic* (Indianapolis: Hackett, 2006).

Rorty, Richard, *Achieving our Country* (Harvard: Harvard University Press, 1998).

Rosen, Stanley, *Plato's Republic: A Study* (New Haven: Yale University Press, 2005).

Rowe, Christopher, 'The Literary and Philosophical Style of the *Republic*', in Santas (ed.) (2006).

Sachs, David, 'A Fallacy in Plato's *Republic*', in Kraut (ed.) (1997).

Sallis, John, *Being and Logos: Reading the Platonic Dialogues*, 3rd edn (Bloomington and Indianapolis: Indiana University Press, 1996).

Sayers, Sean, *Plato's Republic: An Introduction* (Edinburgh: Edinburgh University Press, 1999).

Schleiermacher, Friedrich, *Introduction to the Dialogues of Plato*, trans. William Dobson (New York: Arno, 1974).

Sheppard, D. J., 'Why the Philosopher Returns to the Cave', in *The Richmond Journal of Philosophy*, issue 6, spring 2004.

Sheppard, D. J., 'Plato's Critique of Democracy', in *The Richmond Journal of Philosophy* issue 10, summer 2005.

Strauss, Leo, *City and Man* (Chicago: The Chicago University Press, 1964).

Taylor, C. C. W., 'Plato's Totalitarianism', in Kraut (ed.) (1997).

Vlastos, Gregory, 'Was Plato a Feminist?' in Kraut (ed.) (1997).

Waterfield, Robin, Introduction to and translation of Plato, *Republic* (Oxford: Oxford University Press, 1993).

Weil, Simone, *Intimations of Christianity among the Greeks*, trans. Elisabeth Chase Geissbuhler (London: Routledge and Kegan Paul, 1957).

White, Nicholas P., *A Companion to Plato's Republic* (Indianapolis: Hackett, 1979).

Whitehead, A. N., *Process and Reality* (Cambridge: Cambridge University Press, 1929).

Wilde, Oscar, 'A Few Maxims for the Instruction of the Over-Educated', in *Collins Complete Works of Oscar Wilde* (London: Harper Collins, 1999).

Williams, Bernard, 'The Analogy of City and Soul in Plato's *Republic*', in Kraut (ed.) (1997).

Xenophon, *Conversations of Socrates*, trans. Hugh Tredennick and Robin Waterfield (Harmondsworth: Penguin, 1990).

Index